UNIVERSITY LIBRARY
W. S. U. ▪ STEVENS PO

W9-AOV-834

6.00 AC

THE COMMUNIST PARTY OF VENEZUELA

COMPARATIVE COMMUNIST PARTY POLITICS
Jan F. Triska, Editor

Hoover Institution Studies: 24

THE COMMUNIST PARTY OF VENEZUELA

By Robert J. Alexander

HOOVER INSTITUTION PRESS

Stanford University ● Stanford, California

The Hoover Institution on War, Revolution and Peace, founded at Stanford University in 1919 by the late President Herbert Hoover, is a center for advanced study and research on public and international affairs in the twentieth century. The views expressed in its publications are entirely those of the authors and do not necessarily reflect the views of the Hoover Institution.

Standard Book Number 8179-3241-0 (hard); 8179-3242-9 (paper)
Library of Congress Catalog Card Number: 77-77320
©1969 by the Board of Trustees of the Leland Stanford Junior University
All rights reserved
Printed in the United States of America

JL
3898
.C6
A67

TO AUGUSTA HOLMES POWELL

199323

193529

CONTENTS

PREFACE

During the last twenty years I have been interested in the activities of the Communist Party of Venezuela. During visits to that country between 1947 and 1961, I was able to talk on many occasions with various Communist leaders, on both a national and local level. On these trips and later, I was able to collect considerable documentary material, much of which is cited in this monograph, including publications of the Communist Party itself and of other organizations interested in the party's activities.

Several of my previous writings have concerned Venezuela. These include an extensive study of the Betancourt regime published in 1964, a chapter on Rómulo Betancourt in my volume *Prophets of the Revolution,* and a chapter dealing with the Venezuelan Communists in *Communism in Latin America.* I therefore was pleased to receive the invitation of Professor Jan F. Triska to contribute a study of the Venezuelan Communist Party to a series of monographs on non-ruling Communist parties which the Studies of the Communist System of Stanford University was preparing. This work follows a general outline for all the studies prepared under the aegis of the Studies, which explains the particular organizational structure of the present volume.

Because of the special characteristics of the Communist Party of Venezuela, it has been necessary to vary the general outline in one important detail. The most distinctive thing about the Venezuelan Party is its unsuccessful experiment with the violent road to power between 1962 and 1966. Therefore, instead of ending the historical study of the party at 1956, as was originally proposed, I have felt it necessary to carry the historical sketch down to 1966, to include the period of violence and the controversy arising around the issue of withdrawal from the guerrilla war. I have thus divided this section of the volume into two parts: one covers the period between the foundation of the Partido Comunista de Venezuela (PCV) in 1931 and the overthrow of the Pérez Jiménez dictatorship on January 23, 1958; the other consists of a detailed study of the circumstances leading to the PCV's choice of the violent road to power, the nature of this attempt forcibly to seize power, and the circumstances of the eventual withdrawal from guerrilla activity.

I owe a number of debts of gratitude in connection with the writing of this monograph. In the first place, I want to express my thanks to Professor Triska for inviting me to write the study. I must also thank my graduate student, Sergio Roca, for help in searching out certain statistical material and other data. Finally, I owe much to my wife, Joan, and my children, Tony and Meg, for allowing me to devote the considerable time necessary to write this monograph, time during which I was preoccupied with Venezuela and its Communists, when I am sure they thought I should be paying more attention to them.

R. J. A.

Rutgers University
New Brunswick, N. J.
September 1968

EDITOR'S INTRODUCTION

This study of the Communist Party of Venezuela is one of a series of monographs which together comprise comparative politics of non-ruling communist parties (NRCPs). The series is concerned with the state of the non-ruling communist parties in the world, with the causes of their emergence, and in particular with the question: *Why are NRCPs strong in some national states and not in others?* The theoretical focus of the series is on (a) the *varieties* of the NRCPs and their individual mutations and variations from the prescriptive Bolshevik organizational model; (b) the *causes* of these varieties, and identification of those environments within which NRCPs operate which have been most variety-productive; and (c) the *consequences* of these varieties, i.e., the particular conditions these varieties have produced which make for similarities or differences among the NRCPs.

The series examines three major assumptions:

1) Traditionally, whatever its immediate objectives and preoccupations, every NRCP has professed the principal long-range aspiration of becoming a ruling party, i.e., each has hoped to follow the path of those parties which—like the Czechoslovak, the Yugoslav, the Polish, or the Chinese party—became ruling communist parties (RCPs). However, the less an NRCP is willing to sponsor solely the interests of the RCPs, the more it tends to deviate from this aspiration. Moreover, the peaceful coexistence strategy of the USSR since the Twentieth Congress of the CPSU has not supported the aspiration of the NRCPs to all-out struggle for power in their national states.

2) The NRCPs tend to be progressively more nationally than internationally oriented, and their national orientation tends to increase in direct proportion to the growing disunity among the RCPs (a result, in turn, of the proliferation of RCPs in the world). The NRCPs, in other words, are—like the RCPs—subject to growing positive interaction with their immediate operational environment and hence become progressively less heterogeneous with their national environment. (If an NRCP is small, weak, and operating in an indifferent or hostile national environment, it is probable that its cadres are almost completely alien-

ated from its national environment, and that its perceived operational environment is an extension of that perceived by the ruling communist parties.)

3) The greater the coincidence between means and/or goals of an NRCP and its operational environment, the more influential the NRCP. NRCPs have declined or been unsuccessful in those countries—such as Ireland, Canada, and the United States—where their operational environment has been unalterably hostile; they have gained or been successful in those parts of the world where they have adjusted to their operational environment—as in Italy and France—or where the operational environment has favored NRCP means and/or goals, as in Asia. (NRCPs operating in an unfriendly environment in developing nations and which side with the Chinese Communist Party in advocating uprisings and violence in underdeveloped countries create a danger of general war which the peaceful coexistence policy of the USSR was designed to avoid.)

Among other assumptions examined empirically in the series—some of them current in the various writings on the subject—are the following: "Communism breeds on poverty and underdevelopment"; "The achievements of communism are the achievements of organization"; "Communist ideology is an imperfect theory of modernization"; and "The behavior of an NRCP is determined by its functions within its operational environment."

In the sense that "freedom of formation of associations to seek to control the state prevails only in the Western democracies and in states modeled after them,"[1] the NRCPs are *political parties* in those states where such freedom, however minimal, exists; but even in non-democratic states they have competitors for rule. The NRCPs differ from the RCPs not only in that the ruling parties are not parties at all in the above sense, but they are by definition without competitors for rule. This difference has important consequences: The extant political and social system usually has a far greater impact on an NRCP than on an RCP, while the relative impact of the NRCP on its operational (national) environment is normally incomparably smaller. This difference is observable and measurable in the social composition of the NRCPs; in their structures, operational codes, and strategies; and in their relations with other CPs, both ruling and non-ruling.

What constitutes a communist party? Some communist parties call themselves communist, whereas others, such as the Irish Workers' League, are truly communist in all save name. Still others, such as the Mexican Workers' and Farmers' Party, have strong communist leanings but exist independently of, and sometimes in competition with, the local

1. V. O. Key, Jr., *Politics, Parties, and Pressure Groups*, 2d ed. (New York: Crowell, 1953), p. 223.

communist party. Some countries have both a communist party-states oriented party and a "national" communist party; some countries have these plus a Trotskyite party. Where communism is illegal, numerous left-wing parties may preach Marxist slogans but maintain few connections with the Communist party-states.

We are concerned here only with those parties which perceive themselves to be a part of the world communist movement and are so perceived by the party-states, thus automatically excluding all Trotskyite and "national" communist parties, as well as left-wing parties which do not acknowledge the party-states' leadership. Furthermore, we count only one party per country, selecting that party most closely identified with the communist system.

The common outline divides each study into six principal parts: Chapters I and II concern the historical setting, concentrating on the emergence, evolution, and organizational strength of the NRCP. Here we search for causal relations—why and how an NRCP came into being, which phenomena influenced its evolution; which developments contributed to its strength. Chapter III deals with the NRCP in terms of its role and organization, i.e., its status, membership, and structure. Chapter IV has to do with the NRCP national environment (its geographic and demographic locale, and the prevailing social, political, economic, military, belief, and other relevant systems). The intercourse between the NRCP and its national environment, and hence the past and present national operational code of the NRCP, are treated in Chapter V. Chapter VI deals with the NRCP's international operational code. And Chapter VII stipulates the principal determinants of the NRCP's behavior. In addition, the Introduction to the case study concentrates on what the author believes to be the unique features of his particular NRCP, what distinguishes it from other national parties. The Summary briefly reviews the high spots of the case study, emphasizing causal explanations of the NRCP's emergence, its strength, and its present orientation.

A few additional words concerning some of the components of the outline are in order.

First, there has been no attempt made as yet to span the gaps between models constructed by three authors who have made important theoretical contributions to the study of NRCPs, namely Gabriel Almond,[2] Hadley Cantrill,[3] and Lucian Pye.[4] Chapter III should remedy this deficiency, at least in part, by emphasizing *role* and *status* of the party. The Chapter describes functions of the NRCP which are assumed to signify the (roughly) three states of party development:

2. *The Appeals of Communism* (Princeton: Princeton University Press, 1954).
3. *The Politics of Despair* (New York: Collier Books, 1962).
4. *Guerrilla Communism in Malaya* (Princeton: Princeton University Press, 1956).

1) In developing nations—in non-politicized, non-community societies—revolutionary NRCPs are a dynamic force. Here they perform, in addition to their own unique objectives, the role of socializers toward modernity.[5] Here they feed the aspirations and ambitions of persons frustrated by an economy that cannot accommodate their skills. The high want/get ratio resulting from such economic conditions, we hypothesize, both alienates and brings into the CP those wishing to transform their societies rapidly and make them part of the modern world.

2) In societies where only some segments of the population have not been integrated and incorporated into the social and political system, the NRCPs attempt to integrate alienated (political and social) individuals for articulation of their dissatisfaction and protest. These *sub-cultural* NRCPs, habituated to defending the negative interests of isolated sections of the society, function more as *social* parties than as political parties. Seton-Watson has described what happened when a sub-cultural NRCP left the protest field to enter responsible government in postwar France: The Communists had traditionally viewed the parliament as a useful forum for propaganda, and "it was not easy to discard this mentality. Denunciation and demagogy were easier and more enjoyable than responsibility."[6]

3) Finally, when NRCPs have gone beyond social protest and assumed political responsibility, their deviant and revolutionary character tends to be replaced by legitimacy and social plausibility, and their difference from other political parties tends to be reduced, sometimes to zero. From an ideological protest movement, the *electoral* NRCP tends to become a pragmatic and non-heretic political force. Italian and French CPs are probably the outstanding examples of NRCPs in this stage of operation.

Chapter III also focuses on status: Is the NRCP *influential?* (What is its political weight?) Is it *militant?* (Has a militant politics normally farther-reaching consequences within the immediate political process?) Is it *tolerated?* (Might the same NRCP be perceived as radical in one system and conservative in another?) Is it *changing* its status? (What are the NRCP elite's present aspirations as compared to those of yesterday? How flexible is the elite's perception of its own role? Could an NRCP typology rank-order NRCPs according to their willingness to experiment and change their organizational forms?) And what are its *prospects?* (Does the NRCP "have a future"?) Inasmuch as all these variables have negative counterparts, twenty different combinations are possible, from one extreme (influential, militant, tolerated, changing NRCPs with positive prospects) to the other (non-influential [impotent],

5. Pye, *op. cit.,* p. 344; Hugh Seton-Watson, *From Lenin to Khrushchev* (New York: Praeger, 1961), p. 320.
6. Seton-Watson, *ibid.,* p. 294.

bargain-oriented, not tolerated, unchanging NRCPs with negative prospects).

With appropriate indicators, the several NRCP types may be of research value in further refining the NRCP types in the world and then matching the differences with (a) the kind of membership-leadership, rank and file, and supporters they attract; (b) socialization processes within the NRCPs; (c) environmental conditions as correlated with party transition from one type to another; etc.

As to the structure of the NRCP: Scholars (Duverger)[7] often assume that CPs are rigid hierarchial orders, that the party occupies the whole time of its elites, and that the party organization does not allow its members to participate fully in ordinary ways in the wider social community. Party demands create a rigid personality type, and the party recruits personalities predisposed to fit easily into the party order.

But is this true of the new parties whose leaders were recruited at the end of the Stalin era and have no personal experience of the Comintern organization in its last years? The major figures in the Cuban party, for instance, all began their party careers in the last years of the Stalin era or later, as did many, perhaps most, of the leaders of sub-Saharan parties, the Burmese party, and many of the newer Latin American parties. It is not possible that these new leaders will diverge from the old stereotype? If they are not rigid authoritarian personalities and if their party organizations are more flexible, leaders now may be more readily responsive to environmental influences than were those of the Stalinist period. New parties with youthful leadership also should be more eclectic in their regard for the history of the CPSU, the Comintern, etc., and more willing to experiment with new strategies and new relationships with other political groups. The Sino-Soviet split should foster such eclecticism.

Chapter IV describes attributes in the environment that may make the objective of the NRPC, namely its transformation into an RCP, possible or easy. For instance, is the political system similar in some respects to that in a communist party-state: dictatorial, one-party, controlled press, etc.? Is the economy largely government controlled? Does the environment present problems similar to those solved more or less successfully by the CP in China, in the Soviet Union, or in Yugoslavia? Are the relations between the state and the Soviet Union and/or China, and/or Yugoslavia friendly and conducive to the growth of a local CP organization, or favorable to the growth of non-communist parties and groups that partially imitate Soviet or Chinese organizations and methods?

The social fabric, and in particular the social structure, of a given

7. Maurice Duverger, *Political Parties* (London: Methuen and Co. Ltd., 1954).

country is an important factor affecting the success of an NRCP. If there is little divergence in primordial loyalties within a country, the effectiveness of communist appeal to primordial sentiments is likely to be slight. The more recent difficulties of CPs in the Middle East, for example, might be due in part to shifts in communist appeals from intellectuals to class loyalties in nations relatively lacking in ethnic diversity.

As to the political system, both Max Weber[8] and Duverger have stressed the "natural emergence" of parties, given certain conditions in the political environment of a given state. Weber's formulation of party evolution encompasses as causative factors both the development of a national legislature and the growth in size of the electorate. Duverger, whose work is perhaps more relevant for the study of NRCPs, deals in part with extenally created parties which emerge outside the legislature and invariably pose some sort of challenge to the ruling group, particularly in terms of representation. Duverger also stresses that externally created parties may be associated with (1) expanded suffrage, (2) strongly articulated secular or religious ideologies, or (3) nationalistic or anti-colonial movements. This broader handling of causality is more applicable to a study of NRCPs because their development may well deviate from any general pattern in response to partisan strategies devised by one or more communist party-states.

The concern with party organization (see Chapter V) is widespread in the literature. Sigmund Neuman,[9] for example, postulates that one of the functions of the modern society is to transform parties of individual representation into parties of integration. Duverger's overly complex scheme of party organizations may be contrasted with overly simplified concepts, such as the dichotomous schemes of Thomas Hodgkin ("elite parties" vs. "parties of personalities")[10]; Ruth Schachter ("patron parties" vs. "mass parties")[11]; Martin Kilson ("caucus-type parties" vs. "mass-type parties")[12]; or even John Kautsky ("traditionalist nationalists" vs. "modernist nationalists")[13]. However, such typologies, while useful in ranking parties along a single continuum, are not necessarily useful for our purpose of explaining the relations between en-

8. *The Theory of Social and Economic Organization* (Glencoe: The Free Press, 1947).
9. *Modern Political Parties* (Chicago: University of Chicago Press, 1956).
10. *African Political Parties* (Baltimore: Pelican, 1960).
11. "Single Party Systems in West Africa," *American Political Science Review,* LV (1961), pp. 294-307.
12. "Authoritarian and Single Party Tendencies in African Politics," *World Politics,* XV, No. 2 (January 1963).
13. *Political Change in Underdeveloped Countries* (New York: Wiley, 1962); see also Colin Leys, "Models, Theories, and the Theory of Political Parties," *Political Studies,* VII (1959), pp. 127-46; Neil A. McDonald, *The Study of Political Parties* (New York: Doubleday, 1956); and Charles E. Merriam and Harold F. Grosnell, *The American Party System,* 4th ed. (New York: Macmillan, 1949).

vironmental influences and the changing organizational structures and behavior patterns of NRCPs. Here the linkage between NRCP characteristics and environmental influences are especially important.

A number of creative people have contributed to this series. In addition to the authors of the series, in this case Professor Robert J. Alexander, I would like to thank Wallace Berry, Jack Kangas, Carole Norton, Noralou Roos, John Rue, and Maurice Simon for their imaginative contributions and valuable assistance.

Jan F. Triska

Stanford University
January 1969

AUTHOR'S INTRODUCTION

A study of the Partido Comunista de Venezuela (PCV) is significant for at least four reasons. First, the Venezuelan party is one of three Communist parties in Latin America which in recent years have resorted to the use of force as the road to power (the others are the CPs of Colombia and Guatemala), and the one most completely committed to that strategy. Second, the Venezuelan experience shows how disaster can overtake a Communist party which resorts to force and fails. Third, it indicates the difficulties which a strong democratic leftist party presents for a Communist party. And finally, the Venezuelan case illustrates the degree to which a government of the democratic left, carrying out a program of social reform, economic development, and moderately nationalistic handling of foreign affairs, can undercut the bases of a Communist party.

The Partido Comunista de Venezuela, encouraged and pushed by the Castro regime in Cuba, committed itself unreservedly early in 1962 to using force to achieve power. With its ally, the Movimiento de Izquierda Revolucionaria, it first launched a campaign of urban terrorism, with lesser emphasis on guerrilla war in the rural sector, to overthrow the administration of President Rómulo Betancourt. When that campaign failed (with almost universal participation by the Venezuelan voters in the election of December 1963, the victory went to Acción Democrática [AD], President Betancourt's own party), the Venezuelan Communists did not abandon the strategy of violence; they merely shifted to all-out efforts to wage a guerrilla war.

But by the latter part of 1965, the principal Communist leaders, concluding that this tactic too had failed, decided to withdraw from the struggle. This decision not only created dissidence within the PCV; it also embroiled the party in a bitter polemic with the Communist Party of Cuba, and personally with Fidel Castro.

The second noteworthy aspect of the Venezuelan Communist experience is that it shows the danger a Communist party runs if resort to violence fails. The Venezuelan party was decimated by its attempt to use urban terrorism and guerrilla war. It lost membership, it lost influence in the labor and peasant movements, and it was almost completely isolated from the Venezuelan masses. These results were undoubtedly of major importance in deciding the Venezuelan Communist leaders to abandon the violent road to power, at least for a while, and to attempt to reestablish contacts with the masses.

A third major aspect of the Venezuelan Communist experience is the fact that Acción Democrática, the major party of the democratic left, has been a major stumbling block to the Partido Comunista de Venezuela during most of its existence. Acción Democrática has for nearly thirty years offered the people of Venezuela a program of advanced social reform, a nationalistic program for the key oil industry, advocacy of rapid economic development, and support for political democracy. This program has made AD the largest party in the country since the early 1940's.

The PCV has thus always had AD as its major enemy. Its own policies have in the main depended upon its attitude toward this rival. On several occasions the PCV has faced internal controversy as to whether it should attempt to form a common front with AD, in order to attract the masses of that party, or should offer strong resistance to it. Whichever approach the Communists adopted, Acción Democrática—which has been virtually impervious to Communist blandishments with the exception of a short period in the late 1950's—has constituted a major barrier to Communist progress in Venezuela.

Finally, it must be noted that Acción Democrática has been in power twice: from 1945 to 1948, and from 1959 to the present. During its periods in power it has worked energetically to put its program into effect. It has carried out extensive agrarian reform, has brought about rapid development of both agriculture and industry, has established a nationalistic policy which within the foreseeable future will put the oil industry, fundamental to the national economy, in Venezuelan hands. All this it has done while operating within a constitutional democratic system, unique in the country's history.

The PCV occupies a unique position among the Communist parties of Latin America. There is little doubt that the leadership of other Latin American Communist parties has closely followed the experiences of the Venezuelan party during the last few years, and that consequently the Venezuelan experiences have contributed to a realignment of forces of the extreme left in Latin America. Virtually all orthodox Latin American Communist parties, which are aligned with the Soviet Union, have supported the PCV's decision to withdraw from guerrilla war and seek to recoup what support it once had among the Venezuelan masses.

They have also backed the PCV's declaration of independence from Fidel Castro's suzerainty over the Latin American extreme left. The recent history of the PCV has thus contributed much to the growing breach between the Communist parties of Latin America and the party and regime of Fidel Castro.

THE COMMUNIST PARTY OF VENEZUELA

Chapter One

HISTORY OF THE VENEZUELAN COMMUNIST PARTY

The Partido Comunista de Venezuela was established during the struggle against the dictatorship of Juan Vicente Gómez, famed "tyrant of the Andes." The first Venezuelan Communist groups were founded by individuals who had been exiled by the regime, although none of these expatriate nuclei actually founded a full-fledged Venezuelan Communist party.

In the 1920's a young man named Ricardo Martínez was exiled for opposition to Gómez, and found refuge in the United States. There he joined the Communist Party of the United States. Under its auspices he became a "Latin American expert" for the Communist International. Among other activities, he attended the 1927 Congress of the Pan-American Federation of Labor in Washington, as delegate of a nonexistent Venezuelan labor movement. He took the lead in denouncing the intervention of the United States in Latin American affairs, and was also highly critical of the American Federation of Labor, the United States affiliate of the PAFL.[1] In 1928 he attended the Fifth Congress of the Communist International, and stayed in Moscow for some time thereafter, apparently helping to direct the affairs of the Latin American affiliates of the Comintern.

Another precursor of the Venezuelan Communist Party was Gustavo Machado. He first fell afoul of the

3

Gómez dictatorship in 1914, and spent much of the next twenty years in exile. In the mid-1920's he found refuge in Cuba, where he cooperated with Julio Antonio Mella in founding the Communist Party of Cuba. [2] Subsequently, he made his headquarters in Mexico, where he brought together a group of exiles to form the Partido Revolucionario Venezolano. As its representative he went to Nicaragua, where he spent some time with the rebel forces of General Augusto Sandino, who was carrying on a guerrilla war against the United States Marines then occupying the country. For a while thereafter, he was Sandino's representative in Mexico. [3]

New impetus was given to the formation of a Venezuelan Communist party in 1928. In that year a group of students at the Central University of Caracas revolted against the Gómez dictatorship and seized the presidential palace, but were defeated after several days of demonstrations and skirmishing in the capital.

Most leaders of this student movement were arrested by the regime, and were either exiled or kept in jail. Among the more famous exiles was Rómulo Betancourt, who after some wandering found refuge in Costa Rica. There he participated in founding the Costa Rican Communist Party, to which he belonged until 1935. At that time he left the Communist Party, opposing its leadership's decision to affiliate as a full-fledged member of the Communist International, arguing that Latin American countries should seek their own answers to their problems rather than accepting the dictates of Moscow or any other European center. He was destined to become the Venezuelan Communists' most tenacious and formidable enemy. [4]

FOUNDING OF THE VENEZUELAN COMMUNIST PARTY

It was not until 1931 that the Communist Party of Venezuela was organized on Venezuelan soil. It was established by some veterans of the 1928 uprising who had remained in the country, and its founding meeting was attended by a United States citizen, Joseph Kornfedder, who was then operating as an agent of the Communist International in the northern part of South America.[5] Presumably on Kornfedder's recommendation, the party was first given the status of a "sympathetic" party by the Comintern, and then was accepted as a full-fledged member party by the Seventh Congress of the International in 1935.[6]

So long as Juan Vicente Gómez lived, the Partido Comunista de Venezuela remained underground. Its members and leaders were frequently arrested and not infrequently tortured. It could hold no public meetings or otherwise get its message before more than a few people at a time.

An incident in 1936 demonstrated the degree of control the Comintern exercised over the fledgling party at this time. As reported in the Comintern magazine Communist International of November 1936, the Comintern's International Control Commission had undertaken to expel from the Venezuelan Communist Party three of its leaders, whom the Commission had found guilty of providing Gómecista police with information about fellow party members while under torture. The report noted that the International Control Commission had taken this action because the appropriate organs of the Partido Comunista de Venezuela had refused to do so.

THE PCV UNDER LOPEZ CONTRERAS

In December 1935 Juan Vicente Gómez died in his sleep. His successor, General Eleazar López Contreras, began almost immediately to relax the tight controls of the Gómez dictatorship. Exiles were allowed to return, trade unions and political parties were permitted to organize, controls over the press and other organs of public expression were relaxed.

Among the returning exiles were various people who had joined Communist parties abroad, and among those freed from prison were the young leaders of the Venezuelan Communist Party. Some of these men, joined by others, began almost immediately to enter into contact with the workers, particularly those of the oil fields, around Lake Maracaibo and in parts of Eastern Venezuela. Among the first recruits of the Communists was Jesús Faria, an illiterate oil worker with a keen intelligence and a talent for leadership, who was destined to become one of the party's major leaders.

The hitherto illegal Communists hastened to establish an open party, the Partido Republicano Progresista, one of several groups set up at this time by returning exiles and former underground workers. Others included the Organización Revolucionaria Venezolana (ORVE), * whose principal figure was Rómulo Betancourt; the Unión Nacional Republicano; and the Bloque Nacional Democrático

---

*There is some debate about the meaning of the initials O. R. V. E. John Martz claims that these letters stood for Movimiento de Organización Revolucionaria. However, a number of former ORVE members have given us the name which we use.

which operated principally in the oil state of Zulia around
Lake Maracaibo and included both future Acción Democrática leaders such as Valmore Rodríguez, and future
outstanding Communists such as Juan Bautista Fuenmayor
and Olga Luzardo.

In April 1936 all these groups joined to establish the
Bloque de Abril, as the principal center of opposition to
the López Contreras regime. The united opposition was
very critical of the new Labor Law enacted by the regime,
which they accused of being designed more to control organized labor than to foster it. They also were strongly
opposed to the new constitution enacted by López Contreras, which maintained the former system of indirect
election, whereby the citizenry directly elected only city
councilmen, who in turn elected Congressmen, who chose
the President of the Republic.

Most participating groups conceived the formation of
the Bloque de Abril as a first step toward establishing a
single party, which finally took place on October 28, 1936.
The party was named Partido Democrático Nacional. All
pre-existing left-wing groups except the Unión Nacional
Republicana were represented in the founding meeting of
the PDN. [7]

Two factors hindered the progress of the Partido
Democrático Nacional: governmental opposition and internal dissension. The new party applied for official recognition as a legal political party. However, after some
hesitation, the executive authorities turned down the application on the grounds that the group was controlled by
Communists; an appeal to the Supreme Court was rejected.
A subsequent attempt by some of the PDN people to establish another legal party, the Partido Venezolano Democrático (not to be confused with the party of the same
name established several years later by President Medina

Angarita), was also rejected, because some of the applicants for recognition of the PDN had also signed the application for legalization of the new party. [8]

Thus the Partido Democrático Nacional was never recognized under that name as a legal party. An even greater handicap was the internal feuding which started as soon as the PDN was founded. The non-Communists insisted that the Communists abandon their old organization, meld completely with the new party, and break all connections with the Communist International. This, naturally, the Communists refused to do, with the result that soon after the party was established the Communists abandoned the PDN, and the people who had originally established the ORVE continued to function under the name Partido Democrático Nacional. [9]

In March 1937 the López Contreras government suppressed all opposition. Most leaders of radical groups were arrested and the majority were deported. Among the non-Communists, only Rómulo Betancourt and Alejandro Oropeza Castillo escaped capture until 1940. The Communists were luckier; many of their important leaders had recently returned from training abroad, and were therefore unknown to the government and escaped detection by the police. [10]

During this period the Communists were able to dominate the labor movement. They were particularly strong among the oil workers, in whose organization they had pioneered. Their attempt to establish a confederation of workers in January 1937 was broken up by the government, but many local unions existed in the oil fields and in the major cities, and the Communists succeeded in controlling a majority of them in these early years.

THE COMMUNISTS AND MEDINA ANGARITA

When López Contreras' presidential term expired in 1941 he decided to obey his own 1936 constitution, which forbade the immediate reelection of the president, and to turn the office over to someone else. He chose as his successor another military man, like him a native of the mountain state of Táchira in western Venezuela, General Isaías Medina Angarita.

The Communists were among those opposed to the election of General Medina, but their opposition was little more than symbolic, since the naming of Medina by the Congress, which was completely controlled by the out-going president, was assured. However, the Partido Democrático Nacional decided to name the famous novelist Rómulo Gallegos, one of the few PDN-backed members of the Chamber of Deputies, as their "symbolic" nominee for the presidency. The Communists also backed the candidacy of Gallegos. [11]

On the day that Congress named General Medina Angarita the new president, the Communists organized a demonstration outside the Capitol in the heart of Caracas. Marchers carried signs denouncing the president-to-be as a "fascist" and otherwise made very clear their opposition. However, President Medina surprised everyone. Instead of continuing the kind of relatively bloodless but firm dictatorship which López Contreras had presided over during his later years in the presidency, the new chief executive took a democratic tack. He organized his supporters into a new party, the Partido Democrático Venezolano, and its ranks were joined by such figures as novelist and businessman Arturo Uslar Pietri, who became a member of the Medina government, and Jóvito Villalba, a leader of the Students Federation in 1936 and a founder of ORVE, who was a PDV senator during the Medina period.

In other ways, too, Medina indicated his democratic bona fides. He had the constitution amended to provide for direct election of members of Congress, instead of their selection by electoral colleges composed of members of municipal councils. Another amendment repealed the constitutional provision which had specifically outlawed the Communist Party.

Moreover, the opposition was allowed to function with a wide degree of freedom. The exiles were permitted to return, and to organize open political parties. The Partido Democrático Nacional was rechristened Acción Democrática and in September 1941 was granted legal recognition. The Communists at about the same time were permitted to establish a legal party under the name Unión Popular.

The Venezuelan Communists responded to Medina's overtures by offering him their support. This change in attitude on their part should not be seen only in terms of the Venezuelan national situation, however: it was the general line of the Communist parties in Latin America, after June 21, 1941, to support any regime, democratic or dictatorial, which declared itself on the side of the Allies. Medina gave full political support to the anti-Axis cause.

The extent to which the Communists rallied to President Medina Angarita aroused opposition among party members and those close to the party. Indeed, some years later Juan Bautista Feunmayor, who during the Medina regime was the principal leader of the Communist Party and the chief architect of its alliance with the regime, told the author that he felt the party had perhaps gone too far in its endorsement of the Medina government.

The opposition within Communist ranks found expression in Unión Popular, the "front group" of the Partido

Comunista. The opponents of the pro-Medina stand held
a majority in the National Executive Committee of Unión
Popular. They included such figures as the Machado brothers, Gustavo and Eduardo, Rodolfo Quintero, a leading
trade unionist of the party, and three important trade union
leaders who had been expelled from the Communist Party
in 1940 but had been allowed to join and play a leading part
in Unión Popular, Luis Miquilena, Horacio Scott, and
Cruz Villegas.

The dissidence within Unión Popular reached a high
point in 1944. At a public meeting, Juan Bautista Fuenmayor was booed by members of the opposing faction, and
when he protested this treatment before the National Executive Committee of Unión Popular, that body upheld his
opponents. As a result, Feunmayor and those associated
with him withdrew from Unión Popular and launched their
own Partido Comunista, which early in 1945 was given
government recognition as a legal political party. At
about the same time the Unión Popular leaders, who had
"expelled" Feunmayor and his group, renamed their party
the Partido Comunista   Unitario. [12] Following this split
in the ranks, the two Communist groups continued to follow different lines toward the Medina government. The
Partido Comunista remained on friendly terms with the
regime, while the Unión Popular-Partido Comunista
Unitario frankly opposed it.

The Communists suffered another major setback
during the Medina Period when, in March 1944, the Second Workers Congress convened to establish a national
labor confederation. The Congress had been called, and
was attended by, Vicente Lombardo Toledano, head of
the Confederation of Workers of Latin America. Leaders
of trade unions under both Communist and Acción Democrática were in attendance, and a bitter power struggle
between the two political blocs developed.

Adeco (Acción Democrática) delegates set a trap into which their Communist opponents—whether from over-confidence or inexperience, the author does not know—fell quickly. During a discussion concerning elections for the executive committee of the new confederation, an AD-affiliated delegate arose to propose that since two political groups were represented at the meeting, the executive committee should be equally divided between them. An angry Communist delegate arose to protest, arguing that since the Communists were clearly in a majority, they should have a majority on the new committee. When this position was endorsed by a vote of the delegates, those affiliated with Acción Democrática withdrew from the Congress.

This debate provoked the government of Medina Angarita into prompt action. At a special cabinet meeting on the evening of the day the AD trade unionists withdrew, it was decided that because the Congress had openly supported a political party, an action which was forbidden by the Labor Law, all further sessions would be suspended. Moreover, the cabinet voted to cancel the legal recogni tion of all unions represented by delegates who had stay in the Congress after the minority's withdrawal.

This decision paved the way for Acción Democrática to capture control of the Venezuelan labor movement. In the process of reorganizing the unions whose legal recognition had been cancelled, Acción Democrática succeeded in capturing control of a sizable number, enough to claim a comfortable majority in the labor movement as a whole. It remains something of a mystery why President Medina Angarita acted as he did on this occasion. It was cer-tainly a political mistake from his point of view: the Communists were at that time his closest allies, while Acción Democrática represented a strong and militant opposition. It would seem he had nothing to gain and everything to lose by facilitating the seizure of control of organized labor by the major opposition party.[13]

THE "UNITY CONGRESS" AND CONTINUED DIVISION

The transfer of control of the labor movement to Acción Democrática undoubtedly helped prepare the way for the overthrow of the Medina government. Its ouster was precipitated by the problem of presidential succession. As the end of President Medina's term approached, Acción Democrática urged him to have the constitution amended to provide for popular election of his successor. When General Medina refused, they suggested that the government and the opposition agree on a common candidate.

The president at first accepted this suggestion, and he and Acción Democrática agreed to support the Venezuelan Ambassador to Washington, Diogenes Escalante. A group of AD leaders visited the United States, and received Escalante's assent to his candidacy. However, soon afterward he fell ill and was forced to withdraw from the race.

It proved impossible for the president and the opposition to reach agreement on a substitute for Escalante, and Medina went ahead with plans to have Congress elect a relatively obscure lawyer of his own choice. As a result, Acción Democrática accepted the invitation of a group of young army officers to participate in a coup against the Medina government, the planning for which was already far advanced.

This coup was executed successfully on October 18, 1945. By agreement between the young officers and the Acción Democrática chiefs, seven of the nine members of the new Junta Revolucionaria government were civilians, and six of these were members of AD. Rómulo Betancourt became head of the Junta and, in effect, Provisional President of the Republic.

At first, both groups of Communists opposed the October 18 coup. When the Fuenmayor Communists of the Partido Comunista de Venezuela learned that the uprising was engineered by Acción Democrática instead of by ex-President López Contreras, as they had first imagined, they withdrew their opposition. However, the other Communist group, the Partido Comunista Unitario, fought in the streets beside army elements loyal to Medina until they were defeated. Some of them were jailed for several days after the coup.

The split in the Communist ranks continued under the Acción Democrática regime. Each party sought recognition from the new government as the legal Communist Party. The Fuenmayor group held its Fifth Congress in February 1946, and nominated a list of candidates, headed by Juan Bautista Fuenmayor, for the Constituent Assembly elections which the Betancourt regime had called. This Congress also expressed qualified support for the new government, applauding certain of its "progressive acts."[1]

The other Communist group, now known popularly as the "Machamiques" (from the names of its principal leaders, Gustavo Machado and Luis Miquilena) on the other hand strongly opposed the Betancourt government, as they had opposed its predecessor. They used their influence in the labor movement to call strikes designed to embarrass the new regime. They also brought about a scission in the AD-controlled Federation of Workers of the Federal District by splitting away from the Federation unions under their influence.[15]

But in spite of their differing attitudes toward the Betancourt regime, the two Communist factions did at-

14

tempt to reestablish a united party. To this end, they finally named a joint list of candidates for the Constituent Assembly elections, and succeeded in electing Juan Bautista Fuenmayor of one group and Gustavo Machado of the other to that body.

A Preparatory Committee for a Unity Congress was established, representing the Fuenmayor group, the Machamiques, and a number of independent Communists who were outside both factions. The efforts of this Committee bore fruit in a Unity Congress which met in November 1946. Although it did not succeed in fully unifying the Communists of Venezuela, this Congress did bring about the merger of the Fuenmayor faction, the independents, and some of the Machamiques—notably the two Machado brothers—into a new party.

The Unity Congress was attended by impressive delegations from foreign Communist parties, including those of the United States, Cuba, the Dominican Republic, Mexico, Colombia, Spain, and Catalonia. That the new Communist Party was endorsed by the international Communist movement, is indicated in a letter dated June 23, 1947, from William Z. Foster, President of the Communist Party of the United States, to Juan Bautista Fuenmayor, Gustavo Machado, and Luis Emire Arrieta, in which Foster complimented them on "establishing a united Communist movement in Venezuela."[16]

The dissident group, led by Luis Miquilena and Rodolfo Quintero, continued to function as a second Communist Party. They took the name Partido Revolucionario Proletario (Comunista), and because for the elections in 1947 for President and Congress they adopted black as their identifying color, they were soon known as the Black Communists. The Partido Comunista de Venezuela, inaugurated at the Unity Congress, on the other hand, adopted red as their color and were called popularly the Red Communists.

The necessity for all parties to adopt distinguishing colors for electoral purposes stemmed from the electoral law adopted early in 1946 by the Acción Democrática regime. This law granted the right to vote to all citizens over 18 whether or not they could read and write and required each party to be identified on the ballot with a color for easy recognition by voters who could not read. Acción Democrática chose white, the new Christian Social Copei party green, and the new Unión Republicana Democrática party maroon.

ACCOMPLISHMENTS OF THE ACCIÓN DEMOCRÁTICA REGIME

Continued disunity was by no means the principal factor to weaken the Venezuelan Communists during the three years Acción Democrática remained in power. The most serious impediment was the program carried out by the AD government.

On his return to Venezuela in 1936, Rómulo Betancourt had taken the lead in establishing the kind of party he was advocating when, in 1935, he resigned from the Costa Rican Communist Party because of its insistence upon becoming a disciplined member of the Communist International. His goal was to create a socially inclined nationalist party that would cut across class lines to find specifically Venezuelan answers to Venezuela's problems. The Partido Democrático Nacional, converted in 1941 into Acción Democrática, was this party.

Acción Democrática proclaimed itself a multi-class party, trying to rally the country's urban workers, peasantry, and intellectuals behind a nationalist, anti-imperialist, democratic, and socially advanced program. It sought to put this program into practice after October 18, 1945.

The petroleum problem was one of the first that the Betancourt government tackled. The government program had urged as a national objective a policy that would secure for Venezuela the greatest return possible from the exploitation of its most important natural resource, and to invest this income in ways that would improve the levels of living of the people and develop the national economy.

Soon after October 18, the new government and the foreign oil companies comprising the oil industry entered into negotiations which resulted in the famous "50-50" policy. Legislation was enacted to provide Venezuela 50 per cent of the oil companies' gross profits. If government income derived from royalties, normal income tax, and municipal taxes amounted to less than this sum, the companies and the Ministry of Mines and Petroleum were to hold year-end consultations to determine how the companies should make up the delinquency—whether by direct tax payment or by investment in housing or some other social project mutually agreed upon. The Acción Democrática government also adopted the basic principles that no new concessions should be granted to foreign oil companies, and that any further land grants for petroleum exploitation should be to a government oil company, yet to be established.

The new petroleum policy vastly increased the government's financial resources. Government income rose from an average of 350 million bolivares between 1938 and 1945, to 1,315 million in 1947.[17] This greatly augmented income went into a variety of programs and projects.

For instance, the regime made an effort to deal with

17

the emergency situation in the transport system, particularly in the city of Caracas. Large numbers of second-hand buses were imported to supplement the much older ones used in the capital. The writer remembers seeing in 1947, in Caracas, a bus that once belonged to the Public Service Corporation of New Jersey, his home state, as yet unpainted for its new operations.

Some of the increased revenue was spent to counteract the threat of inflation then hanging over the country. To this end, prices of foodstuffs and inexpensive clothing used by the poor were held down by government subsidy. [18]

The regime made particularly notable progress in the fields of education, health, and housing. The number of children in primary schools increased from 131,000 in 1945 to 500,000 in 1948. [19] The number of students enrolled in secondary schools rose from 11,500 in 1945 to 22,000 in 1948. [20] University attendance increased from 2,940 students in 1945-46, to 4,586 in 1947-48. [21]

The AD regime put special emphasis on expanding the education of teachers. Seven new government normal schools were opened, and their enrollment increased from 1,200 in 1945 to 4,500 in 1948. [22]

The Ministry of Health launched a broad program for making medical facilities more readily available to the poorer segments of the populace; several new hospitals were built between 1945 and 1948. [23] The social security system, which at that time provided principally health insurance, was extended beyond Caracas, where it had originally been established, to several cities of the interior.

The housing program, which had been started hesitatingly during the Medina regime with a relatively limited number of high-rise apartments, was expanded and reformed under Betancourt, whose government adopted the policy of constructing small apartment buildings or individual houses. The government also built housing in various provincial cities, instead of concentrating its efforts only in Caracas. During the first two years of the AD regime, the Banco Obrero built twice as many low-cost houses as it had constructed in the previous sixteen years of its existence. [24]

In an effort to come to grips with the latifundia problem, one of the country's most pressing social issues, the AD government confiscated sizable landholdings from ex-President Medina and former officeholders in his administration, on the charge that the holdings had been acquired illegally. Some of these lands, and also some which had been seized earlier from the estate of the late dictator Juan Vicente Gómez, were distributed among peasants working on them. In early 1948, the constitutional regime of President Rómulo Gallegos enacted a general Agrarian Reform Law to push forward this program in a regularized fashion.

The Acción Democrática government also followed policies exceedingly favorable to the organized labor movement. The Ministry of Labor encouraged the establishment and legal recognition of trade unions, and the use of collective bargaining as the principal means of settling differences between employers and their workers. Thus, for instance, the first national collective agreement in the petroleum industry was reached early in 1948, and at the time AD rule was overthrown, 575 collective agreements were in effect in all branches of the economy. [25] The number of unions registered with the Ministry of Labor rose from 252 in 1945 to 1,014 in 1948. About half of the new organizations recognized by the Ministry in this period were peasant unions, a type of labor organization which had been virtually nonexistent until the advent of the AD regime.[26] The number of organized workers increased from between 40,000 and 50,000 at the time of the October 18 coup to about 300,000 in June 1948.[27]

Acción Democrática party influence in organized labor was overwhelmingly predominant during this period. Under the leadership of AD elements, state federations of labor were formed in each of the twenty states, and various national federations were either formed or strengthened. This organizational process culminated in formation of the Confederación de Trabajadores de Venezuela (CTV) at a congress which met in November 1947 in Caracas. The Secretary General of the CTV was AD trade union leader P. B. Pérez Salinas.[28]

In addition to these efforts to raise the standards of living and the health and cultural levels of the populace, the Acción Democrática regime devoted a large proportion of the government's increased revenues to attempts to stimulate diversification of the economy. They contended that the nation's oil wealth was an exhaustible resource, and that it was therefore essential to develop agriculture, mining, and manufacturing, so that when the oil boom ended the country would still have an economy capable of supporting the populace.

The most important government institution for diversification was the Corporación Venezolana de Fomento (Venezuelan Development Corporation), established in 1946 with the aid of technicians from the Chilean Development Corporation, which during the preceding seven years had carried out a successful diversification program in that country.

Agriculture received the major share of funds from the Venezuelan Development Corporation; special attention was paid to improving production of such products as sugar, rice, meat, milk, and other commodities for domestic consumption. The Development Corporation spent some 48.7 million bolivares in its program to stimulate food production. [29]

However, manufacturing was by no means completely overlooked. The Development Corporation granted loans particularly to fertilizer, textile, shoe, and cement industries. [30]

The lending facilities of the Agricultural and Grazing Bank, an old governmental institution, were also notably increased during the AD period, while the bank's policy was altered to give special attention to the needs of smaller farmers, rather than concentrating on the needs of large landholders, as had generally been the case.

Finally, the Venezuelan Development Corporation made available sizable sums for strengthening the infrastructure of the economy. Through its lending activities, output of electricity rose markedly - between 1947 and 1948, for instance, by 21.4 per cent. [31] Construction of roads and highways, and of irrigation works, also increased during the three years of the Acción Democrática government.

Another major achievement was the AD establishment of a full-fledged democratic political regime. Early in 1946 a decree proclaimed elections for a constituent assembly to write a new constitution, and for this purpose the new electoral law already mentioned was enacted.

Under the provisions of this second law, several new parties were established. One of these, which became the major opposition party under the Acción Democrática

regime, was the Partido Social Cristiano Copei.* It was
established and led by a young lawyer, Rafael Caldera,
who had started his political career as a student leader
in the late 1930's. He was Attorney General of Venezuela
during the first month or so of the Betancourt government,
but resigned because of disagreements with the Junta.
The Copei (as it was generally called) professed a Christian Democratic philosophy. During the 1945-48 period,
its major support came from the conservative mountain
states of Táchira, Trujillo, and Mérida, and the party as
a whole was a good deal more conservative than its national leadership.

A second important party established in 1946 was the
Unión Republicana Democrática. An organization of somewhat indistinct ideology, it proclaimed itself during this
period to be "liberal," without defining the term. Its
leadership, and much of its membership, consisted of
people closely associated with the Medina regime, either
as officeholders or otherwise.

Other civilian organizations which prospered during
the three-year period of the Acción Democrática rule included various professional organizations—lawyers, doctors, journalists, and the like—and groups representing
manufacturers, merchants, and other interest groups.
The strength of these civilian institutions contributed to establishing the basis for a civilian-controlled and oriented
society, in place of the traditionally military- and caudillo-
dominated society which had existed in the first century
and a quarter of national independence.

---

*The word "Copei" is derived from the initials of Comité
  Politico Electoral Independiente, the name of the organizing committee out of which the party developed.

The efforts of Acción Democrática to establish political democracy on a firm basis produced three different sets of elections during the three-year period of the party's rule. Subsequently, the AD leaders concluded that they had called the voters to the polls too often in too short a time, with the result that virtually all three years were taken up with campaigning, and the populace was kept in an almost continuous state of political agitation.

The first election, late in 1946, was for a Constitutional Assembly. When the Assembly had completed its task, there was an election in which the President, members of Congress, and members of state legislatures were chosen. Finally, in 1948 elections were held for municipal councils. All these demonstrated the overwhelming strength of Acción Democrática among the voters while it was in power. Although the party's hold on the voters declined somewhat with each successive election, AD still represented the great majority of the citizenry when it was overthrown in November 1948.

The election for members of the Constituent Assembly gave Acción Democrática some 1,099,691 votes, 78.8% of the total, and 137 of the 160 seats in that body. In the election of December 1947, Acción Democrática's candidate for president, Romulo Gallegos, received 74.4% of the total vote, and its congressional candidates 70.8%, electing 38 of 46 senators and 83 of 110 deputies. Finally, in the municipal elections of May 1948, AD polled 70.1% of the total vote. [32]

THE COMMUNISTS DURING THE ACCIÓN DEMOCRÁTICA REGIME

During the three years that Acción Democrática was in power, the overwhelming popularity of the government party among the workers, peasants, intellectuals, and other groups wooed by both AD and the Communists, was the single most important stumbling block to the advance of the Communists. Neither the Red nor the Black Communists were able to offer much more than token opposition to the AD and its regime.

The two Communist groups adopted different tactics in dealing with Acción Democrática and the government. The Reds, led by Juan Bautista Fuenmayor and Gustavo Machado, assumed an attitude of more or less critical support of the government and the ruling party. The Blacks followed a policy of unmitigated hostility.

This difference of attitude was most noticeable in the labor movement. As we have noted earlier, the Black Communists organized their own Federation of Workers of the Federal District, in opposition to the one controlled by the AD trade unionists. They also established a dual federation in the eastern state of Anzoategui, where they had some influence among the oil workers. Neither of these federations belonged to the Confederación de Trabajadores de Venezuela. [33]

In contrast, the Red Communists generally maintained a more friendly attitude toward the AD trade unions. Most of the unions under the influence of the Reds joined the Confederación de Trabajadores de Venezuela and the variou state and industrial affiliates of that group. Although they had little voice in the direction of these organizations, they maintained their affiliation, apparently on the theory that more was to be gained by association with groups to which the majority of the workers belonged than by establishing other federations and another confederation which at best could be expected to attract only a small percentage of the country's organized workers.

However, in spite of their generally cooperative

24

attitude toward the AD trade unionists, the Red Communists occasionally found it difficult, if not impossible, to keep their unions within the AD-controlled organizations. For example, early in 1948 there was a severe clash between the two groups within the Petroleum Workers Federation over the terms of the new collective agreement which the federation was negotiating with the employers. As a result of this dispute, the AD leaders of the FED-EPETROL expelled the principal Red Communist figures in the organization. The Communists were forced to establish their own group, which they named the Comité de Unidad y Democrácia Sindical. [34] Shortly before the overthrow of the AD government later that year, it seemed likely there would be a general break between the Red Communists and the Adecos in the labor movement.

In the general political field, too, the attitudes of the two Communist parties toward the AD regime differed. Although Red Communist members of Congress, and their speakers on public platforms, criticized various aspects of the government's program—particularly its oil policies—their criticisms were often offered in a tone of trying to improve that which was good but not good enough. [35] They conceded both publicly and in private conversations that the AD regime had in some areas of its activities been "progressive."[36]

The Partido Revolucionario Proletario (Comunista) attitude was a good deal more violent. Their weekly periodical P.R.P. Comunista regularly contained articles which accused the administration of "betraying" the national interests of the country, and of "oppressing" the workers. The only group toward which the Black Communists were more vituperative was the Red Communists, to whom they referred with fair regularity as "the traitors."

However, neither the attempts of the Reds to cooperate with the AD regime nor the violent opposition of the Blacks was effective in increasing Communist political strength. This was demonstrated by their showing in the elections held between 1946 and 1948.

In the 1946 election for the Constituent Assembly, a united Communist ticket received only 51,179 votes from a total of 1,390,263, and succeeded in electing only two of the 160 members of the Assembly. [37] In the 1947 presidential election, in which the Reds ran Gustavo Machado for chief executive, the Partido Comunista de Venezuela polled only some 40,000 votes; in the concurrent congression: poll they elected only one senator, the oil workers' leader Jesús Faria, and two deputies, Juan Bautista Fuenmayor and Gustavo Machado. The Partido Revolucionario Proletario (Comunista) did not run a presidential candidate, and elected none of its nominees to Congress in polling about 20,000 votes. [38] Finally, in the municipal elections of May 1948, the Reds did elect some city council members in Caracas, in the cities of the central states, and in the oil centers around Lake Maracaibo. The Blacks elected a handful of municipal councilors in the eastern state of Anzoátegui. [39]

THE PERÉZ JIMÉNEZ REGIME

On November 24, 1948, the overthrow of the Acción Democrática government of President Rómulo Gallegos by a military coup marked the beginning of more than nine years of military dictatorship.

These nine years may be divided into two, perhaps three, separate periods. Between November 24, 1948, and December 2, 1952, the government was in the hands of a military junta (Junta Militar); until November 1950, when he was assassinated, Colonel Carlos Delgado

Chalbaud, Minister of War under President Gallegos, presided. After December 2, 1952, the head of the government was Colonel Marcos Peréz Jiménez, who had been chief engineer of the coup against President Gallegos and who was the eminence gris of the Junta after the death of Delgado Chalbaud.

During the period of Colonel Delgado Chalbaud's control of the government—although Acción Democrática and the Red Communist Party were outlawed, the peasant movement was largely destroyed, and the urban labor movement was severely persecuted—the regime continued but did not expand most of the economic and social programs initiated by Acción Democrática. Also, the Copei and URD parties were permitted to function more or less freely.

Late in 1952 the Junta Militar made the mistake of allowing an election for a new Constituent Assembly. The URD and Copei participated in this campaign as opposition parties. The government organized its own party, the so-called Frente Electoral Independiente (FEI). After some hesitation, Acción Democrática threw its support behind the Unión Republicana Democrática. When the election returns showed the URD running far ahead of the government party and Copei also receiving a large percentage of the vote, counting of ballots was suspended. The top leaders of URD were arrested and exiled, and on December 2 Colonel Pérez Jiménez announced he was taking over the presidency "in the name of the armed forces."

From then on, the regime was a personal dictatorship of Colonel (soon self-promoted to general) Pérez Jiménez. It was one of the most ruthless and cruel dictatorships in Latin America in the twentieth century. All political parties were suppressed, thousands of people

27

were jailed, and some shipped off to concentration camps in the Orinoco River Valley, the labor movement all but disappeared, no opposition press or public assembly was permitted. Secret police assassinated opponents not only in Venezuela but outside the country as well.

The regime was almost unbelievably corrupt. President Pérez Jiménez and his associates were reported to have stolen hundreds of millions of dollars, while bribes became the rule rather than the exception for those doing business with the government. Magazines in the United States and elsewhere carried lurid accounts of the importation of girls from other Latin American countries and from Europe to participate in orgies held by the dictator and his friends.

Even more serious in the long run was the government waste of billions of dollars at a time when the oil industry was bringing into the country unprecedented amounts of foreign exchange. Although roads were built and giant housing projects were constructed in Caracas and other cities during the last two years of the regime, vastly greater sums were spent on sumptuous pyramid-building kinds of public works. Among these were the world's most expensive officers club, a hotel designed to afford a sweeping view of Caracas but built on a mountain shrouded in clouds most of the time, and a gigantic shopping center featuring a series of movie theaters all showing the same film but each on a different presentation schedule (so that a visitor could view the film from the beginning no matter when he arrived).

The government made little effort to use oil resources—bolstered by increased funds as a result of its decision to grant new oil concessions to foreign firms—to diversify the economy, to expand agriculture and industry as a basis for a more stable economy than that provided by exploitation of oil resources. Nor was any serious attempt made to use these huge funds for directly improving the living standards of the people.

RED AND BLACK COMMUNIST UNION
ACTIVITY UNDER PÉREZ JIMÉNEZ

As had been the case in the two previous governments, the Red and the Black Communists reacted differently toward the Pérez Jiménez dictatorship. The Junta Militar, although it outlawed Acción Democrática a few days after the coup which ousted President Gallegos, apparently hoped to get along with both Communist groups. The Reds rejected the government's overtures after some hesitation, whereas the Blacks were still collaborating with the regime as late as 1955.

For several years the Reds joined forces with Acción Democrática in the trade union field. The Junta outlawed the Confederación de Trabajadores de Venezuela and the AD-controlled Federation of Workers of the Federal district. (Another Federation of the same name under Black Communist control was untouched.) As a result, the unions led by Acción Democrática and those run by the Red Communists set up separate headquarters, although they worked together on a number of issues. The most dramatic example of this cooperation took place in February 1950, when a labor dispute in the oil fields sparked a general strike in that region, in which unions controlled by both factions participated. The immediate result of this strike, which failed, was that the Federation of Petroleum Workers was outlawed and all oil unions belonging to the federation forfeited legal recognition. The Partido Comunista de Venezuela was also outlawed by the Junta Militar as a direct result of the walkout. [40]

During the remaining years of the dictatorship, both

29

Red Communist and Acción Democrática trade-union groups were severely persecuted. However, the major burden, both of opposition to the regime and of governmental persecution, fell upon Acción Democrática as the country's major democratic party.

The Black Communists collaborated with the Junta Militar and subsequently with the Pérez Jiménez administration almost up to the time the regime was overthrown. This collaboration, again, was particularly visible in the trade-union field.

The Federation of Workers of the Federal District, which was under control of the Black Communists, applied for legal recognition soon after the Junta seized power. Recognition was quickly granted. Moreover, the two regional labor federations under Black Communist control—those of the Federal District and of the state of Anzoátegui—and groups of unions under Black Communist domination in other areas, continued to function openly and with no particular harassment from the military dictatorship at least as late as 1955.

For instance, the Caracas newspaper El Nacional of January 30, 1952 reported on a congress in Barquisimeto of all the labor groups under Black Communist control. The Congress, which was preceded by a public meeting attended by 9,000 people, endorsed the "peace" campaign then being carried out by the world Communist movement, and expressed its support for the World Federation of Trade Unions and its Latin American affiliate, the Confederación de Trabajadores de América Latina.

Later that year, the Federation of Workers of the Federal District held a May Day meeting in its headquarters, which reportedly was attended by some 2,000 people.

Unlike the leaders of most other political groups, the heads of the Black Communists were able to leave and enter the country freely. For instance, Rodolfo Quintero attended the Congress of the World Federation of Trade Unions in 1951 and later made an extended visit to Communist Hungary, as a guest of that government. He then re-entered Venezuela without impediment. [41] When, in 1954, Quintero finally left Venezuela more or less permanently, according to the head of the government's trade Union group M. O. S. I. T. it was at the request of the government, lest his presence in Venezuela "embarrass" the regime during the Inter-American Conference held in Caracas early in 1954. He went to Mexico, where he remained as a member of the secretariat of the Confederación de Trabajadores de América Latina until the Pérez Jiménez regime fell. After Quintero's departure, his unions still continued to function without government interference for some time. [42]

During 1952 the Black Communist Federation of Workers of the Federal District was split when two of its important leaders, Luis Miquilena and Cruz Villegas, opposed Rodolfo Quintero's more or less frank support of the government's handling of a problem which had arisen in the oil fields: in 1951 the existing collective contract had expired, and various union groups of different political orientation had attempted to negotiate with the companies for a new contract. But the Junta Militar stepped in, decreed a modest rise in wages, and left all other issues pending.

The factional dispute over this issue reached a climax at a Black federation meeting on May Day 1952. After a quarrel over who could speak at the meeting, Rodolfo Quintero seized the records of the Federation and moved them and the headquarters of the unions under his control to another building, at the same time "expelling" Miquilena and Villegas. Miquilena and Villegas retained control of two important unions of the federation, the transport workers and the mosaic workers, but virtually all the rest remained with Quintero. The Miquilena-Villegas federation had ceased to exist by late 1954.[43]

COMMUNIST POLITICS
UNDER THE DICTATORSHIP

The divergent attitudes of the two Communist factions was also evident in the general political field. The Black Communists, as collaborators with the Junta Militar, and subsequently for some time with Pérez Jiménez, had little but condemnation for Acción Democrática. However, the attitude of the Red party toward AD was somewhat more complex.

The Partido Comunista de Venezuela took a position of open opposition to the governments in power after November 24, 1948. Although Jesús Faria, Secretary General of the Party some years later, said in reporting to the Party's Third Congress in May 1961, that the party had been guilty of ''coup d'etat illusions'' in the period between 1948 and 1950 (apparently indicating that it had been involved in conspiracies against the regime of the time), it was not officially outlawed until May 13, 1950.[44] The Junta Militar accused the party of cooperating with Acción Democrática in an attempted military coup in Barquisimeto and Maracay a few days before.[45]

Jesús Faria has described the activities of the PCV between November 1948 and May 1950 in the following terms: ''The activity of the Party during those years was characterized by the combination of its legal activity, limited by the restrictive rules of the government, and its semi-clandestine or sometimes fully clandestine activity, at the head of the people's struggles against military usurpation, manifested in student and worker strikes, in the preparation and realization of the great petroleum strike of 1950, in contacts and concurrence with the other clandestine opposition, in campaigns for freedom of political prisoners, freedom of the press, against the sending of prisoners to El Dorado, etc. "[46]

Thus, there was considerable underground cooperation during this period between the Red Communists and the Acción Democrática. In 1951 this cooperation provoked a new split in Red Communist ranks. Juan Bautista Fuenmayor, Ricardo Martínez, and a number of other Party leaders felt that the Party was too subservient to Acción Democrática; indeed they argued that the major enemy of the Communists was not the Junta Militar but AD itself. They were particularly critical of cooperation between the two groups in the 1950 oil workers strike, arguing that a walkout at that time was inopportune because of the depressed state of the world petroleum market, and further that the strike was essentially an AD attempt to debilitate the regime which, if successful, would help the AD seize power once again. The upshot of this bitter quarrel was the expulsion of Juan Bautista Fuenmayor and his associates from the Party. Jesús Faria, the Communist oil workers leader, who was then in prison, was elected Party secretary general in his place. [47]

The Communist Party held its Sixth Conference in April 1951, eleven months after it was outlawed. This meeting, according to Faria, "had the characteristics of a Congress of the Party."[48] It elected a new Central Committee, and of this group Faria comments: "In the Central Committee, alongside the veteran leaders of the I and II Congresses, were elected new elements, proved in the latest combats. This Central Committee has the historic merit of having led the Party in the most dramatic and difficult years of its activity in three decades. It knew how to consolidate the unity of our ranks. It enriched with its action and its studies of national problems, the theoretical preparation of the Party and its political and organizing experience. It knew how to survive persecution so well that it was the only leadership of any political party which acted without interruption, in the midst of extreme sacrifices during the hardest years of repression."[49]

During the following year and eight months, until the election of November 1952, the Partido Comunista de Venezuela held two Plenums of its Central Committee, the X and XI such meetings. These party gatherings launched the slogan of a United Bloc of the opposition. The X Plenum defined this as "a bloc in which will participate all those who wish to fight for the restitution of constitutional guarantees, freedom of political prisoners, cessation of persecution and elections with the participation of all political forces."[50]

The XI Plenum defined the purposes of the Bloc thus: "We make the United Bloc against a common enemy. That enemy is none other than the military-police dictatorship. . . . All efforts must be directed to defeating the policy of the dictatorship, restricting the terror, reestablishing civil liberties, obtaining total amnesty, forcing the calling of elections with the participation of all political forces. Those are the objectives of the United Bloc."[51]

The PCV in this period made a particular appeal to AD for united action. In December 1951 it issued an appeal to the underground National Executive Committee of AD, urging that the two parties carry out joint action on a common program, but Acción Democrática ignored the appeal.[52] At the same time, in a style by then traditional

34

with Communist parties, the PCV sought to undermine
the leadership of the rival party. This was evident in Communist publications of both the underground in Venezuela
and of exile groups operating abroad.

Among others, the following comment in the April
1951 issue of Patria Nueva, published inside Venezuela
as the organ of the National Executive Commission of
Juventud Comunista, contributed to this campaign of trying to divide Acción Democrática rank and file from its
leaders:

Our Party must unmask seriously and completely the traitorous policy, in favor of the
fomentors of war, of the national-traitor
leaders such as Romulo Betancourt and the
national directors of Acción Democrática,
the right wing and pro-imperialist leaders
of URD, of the Copei Party and of the
Trotskyite groups. . . .

In effect, not to unmask the high leadership
of AD, headed by Betancourt, Carnevali,
Troconis Guerrero, Tovar, Malave Villalba
and Co., not to judge our allies in accordance with the positions their leaders assume
with regard to the problem of Peace, not to
denounce the imperialist agents in the midst
of the popular movement, not to place the
struggle for Peace as a concrete and central
task of democratic unity, not to link closely
the struggle against the military dictatorship with the struggle for Peace, would be
to consciously hinder our mobilization and
that of the people against war.

In October 1950 the organ of the Zulia state section

of the Communist Party, <u>Masas</u>, carried another comment in the same vein but even more explicitly aimed at splitting the AD. An article entitled "The Factionalists and the Military Dictatorship," attributed to one Jesús Hernández, had this to say: "To present Betancourt, the fighting cock of Creole, indiscriminately together with all of Ad, is to play the maneuvering game of Señor Betancourt, who is interested precisely in demonstrating to imperialists that he and AD, as a unified whole, are good servants of imperialisr when really in the midst of AD there are anti-imperialist sectors which do not agree with the pro-imperialist position of Betancourt and Co."

Some time later, in the January 24, 1952, issue of the Venezuelan Communist exile newspaper <u>Noticias de Venezuela</u>, an article entitled "We Build the United Bloc of All Forces Which Oppose the Military Dictatorship and Imperialism" referred to "the subservient attitude toward the military conspirators and petroleum magnates of 'Betancourtism,' which directs and controls important organized contingents of Acción Democrática."

With the seizure of full power by Pérez Jiménez in December 1952, the government intensified its persecution of the Partido Comunista de Venezuela. Between that time and the overthrow of the dictatorship early in 1958, the party was able to hold but two Plenums of the Central Committee, one in 1955 and one in February 1957. Jesús Faria notes that "the lack of periodic meetings of the Central Committee constituted an obstacle to the work of leading the Party. The immense difficulties under which we lived, the need for a better clandestine apparatus of security, and the undervaluation of collective work, were factors which caused the interruption of periodic meetings of the Central Committee."[53]

The XIII Plenum of the PCV held in February 1957,

less than a year before the fall of the Pérez Jiménez regime, summed up the mistakes which the party had made since the overthrow of the Acción Democrática regime. As reported by Jesús Faria, these were the following:54

1. Not having correctly appreciated the true correlation of forces in the country; false appreciation of the whole political panorama of the country

2. Having underestimated the blow received by the democratic and progressive forces on November 24, 1948

3. A sectarian policy which led us to:

    a) Confront many enemies at once and reduce the number of our allies

    b) Attack violently those who indicated a different way out of the situation than that which we proposed

    c) Failure to indicate with certainty and clarity the principal enemy and march with the greatest possible number of allies against that enemy

    d) Attempt to impose our opinions in the mass organizations; failure to use persuasion and conviction

    e) Use of ultra-revolutionary phraseology, a product of our sectarian position which isolated us from the masses

4. This sectarian policy came into conflict with similar positions of other forces and led to a separation of those who opposed the dictatorship

5. Coup d'etat illusions during the period 1948-1950, which hampered the development of organizing work and association with the masses, thus closing other possibilities of struggle.

6.   Not understanding in time the contradictions which abounded in the governmental apparatus

7.   Not preparing the Party sufficiently for clandestine operations

8.   Incorrect use, sometimes of various strategies; underestimation of the struggles for immediate demands of the masses

9.   Exaggerated use of agitation to the detriment of organizing tasks

10.   Traditional errors in the conduct of internal struggles in the Party, such as criticizing excessively those who had committed errors, not guaranteeing or stimulating sufficiently the conflict of opinions, insufficient use of criticism and self-criticism in carrying out the true task of collective leadership, confusing healthy criticism with anti-party positions, not permitting a principled discussion of issues.

Efforts were made during the military dictatorship to bring about the reunification of Venezuelan Communist ranks. In the middle of 1952, the Partido Revolucionario Proletario (Comunista) declared its own dissolution for which Rodolfo Quintero offered the explanation that it would pave the way for reestablishing Communist unity. There appears to have been no formal merger of the two groups in the years that followed; however, some former Black Communist leaders were admitted to the Red party sometime before the fall of the Pérez Jiménez regime. Among these leaders was Cruz Villegas, who emerged after the dictatorship as one of the principal trade-union figures in the Partido Comunista de Venezuela. [55] Luis Miquilena, in contrast, abandoned the Communist ranks entirely: after the ouster of the dictatorship he reappeared as a leader of Unión Republicana Democrática.

THE COMMUNISTS AND THE
FALL OF PÉREZ JIMÉNEZ

The stability of the Pérez Jiménez regime was undermined during 1957, and the way paved for more open and overt opposition than had existed since the 1952 election campaign, by the fact that the dictator's term of office was due to expire early in 1958.

He found himself in a quandary: how could he stay in office and yet avoid risking an election which, even against a puppet opposition, might result in a repetition of the events of 1952?

The opposition attempted to deepen the quandary. After consultation the three major parties, Acción Democrática, Copei, and Unión Republicana Democrática, agreed that if elections were held, all three would support the nomination of Rafael Caldera, head of Copei and the only party chief still living in Venezuela. News of this accord was widely disseminated within the country.[56]

However, Pérez Jiménez devised a somewhat ingenious plan that, for the time being at least, seemed to resolve his problem. He decided to hold a plebiscite in which the voters would be asked to cast "yes" or "no" ballots on the question, "Shall General Marcos Pérez Jiménez remain as president during the next five-year presidential term?" No provision was made for what would happen in case of a negative majority. Although this ploy served Pérez Jiménez' immediate purpose, it was largely responsible for his eventual overthrow. The plebiscite brought the expected result and Pérez Jiménez was overwhelmingly "reelected," but most Venezuelans regarded the whole idea of such a plebiscite as ridiculous. When a dictator becomes a subject of ridicule, the effects can be serious. In this case, large numbers of people, once intimidated by the regime, lost their fear. The plebiscite proved to be the beginning of a fast developing process.

Throughout the month of December 1957, Caracas was the scene of demonstrations, growing in intensity, against the regime. Police and military clashed in the streets with students and workers. Residents of the huge super-block housing developments joined the protests and were particularly active. In addition, proclamations signed by hundreds of leading citizens, including even ex-President Lopez Contreras, demanded reestablishment of democratic constitutional government. These documents were widely distributed among the populace.

On New Year's Eve, the military garrison at Los Teques,* as well as virtually all the Venezuelan Air Force, revolted. The uprising was suppressed, whereupon virtually the entire air force flew off to Colombia.

During the three weeks that followed, growing street disturbances unnerved the dictator to the extent that he reorganized his Army command. He even sacrificed key civilian figures of his regime, including Luis Valenilla Lanz, his Minister of Interior, and Pedro Estrada, Chief of the hated secret police, the Seguridad Nacional, both of whom were sent into exile.

However, all was in vain. On January 21, 1958, the opposition called a general strike, which was signalled by the ringing of church bells throughout the republic. The walkout was supported by both workers and employers; its outcome was that the military leaders presented Pérez

---

*Capital of the state of Miranda about 50 miles south of Caracas.

Jiménez with his passports, and sent him into exile early in the morning of January 23, 1958.

The rising civilian opposition to the dictatorship during these last few weeks was not unorganized; it was backed by the underground organizations of Acción Democrática, Copei, Unión Republicana Democrática, and the Partido Comunista de Venezuela. The central organization for this final push against the Pérez Jiménez regime was the so-called Junta Patriotica. It was a subsidiary organ of the Junta Patriotica, the General Strike Committee founded early in January 1958, that organized and carried through the strike.[57]

The first step toward formation of the Junta Patriotica had been taken when, in April 1957, the student followers of Copei, AD, the URD, and the PCV in the Central University of Caracas formed a united Frente Universitario and issued a call for the overthrow of the Pérez Jiménez regime. Then in July 1957 came an initiative by the underground leaders of URD and PCV to establish a similar organization on a national level. This move launched the Junta Patriotica, presided over by URD underground leader Fabricio Ojeda, and made up of representatives of all four parties.[58]

Meanwhile, the exiled leaders of the three non-Communist parties, AD, Copei, and URD, had formed another front of their own. In November 1957, Rómulo Betancourt, Jóvito Villalba of URD , and representatives of Copei issued a joint declaration from New York against the Pérez Jiménez regime and its plebiscite. Then, when Rafael Caldera was exiled in early January, he joined Betancourt and Villalba in signing a Joint Action Pact, a document that not only promised unified action against the dictatorship, but also pledged the parties to maintain their unity after its overthrow. The Communists were

41

pointedly excluded from this agreement.

Thus, while the underground organizations of the non-Communist parties and their exiled leaders diverged somewhat in attitude, within Venezuela the Communists worked closely with members and leaders of the other parties.

THE PROVISIONAL GOVERNMENT

With the fall of the Pérez Jiménez dictatorship, a Junta de Gobierno was established as the provisional government of the Republic. The Junta was at first composed entirely of military men, but it was reorganized within days when two officers resigned and were replaced by two civilian businessmen. Thereafter, although the personnel of the Junta changed several times during its fourteen months in power, it always contained both military and civilian members. When Admiral Wolfgang Larrazábal, the first President of the Junta, resigned to run for the constitutional presidency, his place went to Dr. Edgardo Sanabria, who remained in office until the inauguration of the constitutional regime in February 1959.

In addition to its basic task of paving the way for a return to democratic constitutional government, the provisional government was faced with a wide range of emergencies arising from unpaid debts of the Pérez Jiménez regime, inadequate government revenues, demands for agrarian reform, and several attempted military coups.

During its last several years in office the Pérez Jiménez dictatorship had fallen farther and farther behind in its payments for pyramid-style public works. In lieu of payment, Venezuelan creditors received short-term promises to pay, which in many cases were promptly sold to North American speculators headquartered in leading Caracas hotels. The speculators in turn resold

42

the Venezuelan debt to purchasers in the United States, particularly in New York. These short-term debts totaled at least a billion dollars by the time the Pérez Jiménez regime came to an end. When the dictatorship fell, hordes of creditors presented their paper to the new Venezuelan government for immediate payment. After temporary hesitation, the Larrazábal government decided to pay, rather than to refund short-term debts into long-term bonds as some political leaders and economists urged.

One immediate effect of this sudden payment of a large amount of foreign currency was a drastic reduction of Venezuela's foreign exchange reserves. This effect was intensified by the concurrent withdrawal of sizable amounts of private capital from the country, both by Venezuelans and by foreign investors. Fear was expressed that the long-term stability of the Venezuelan currency would be endangered.

The foreign exchange situation was but one aspect of the economic crisis which descended on Venezuela in 1958. In part, this crisis was the delayed reaction to the declining income from petroleum which resulted when the rush for new oil concessions ended in 1955-56; in part it was caused by a decreased foreign demand for petroleum which, as it happened, coincided almost exactly with the fall of Pérez Jiménez. It was further provoked by the Provisional Government's suspending most of the dictatorship's public works projects, and thereby terminating the sumptuous expenditures, largely concentrated in Caracas, which had supported a real estate boom and generated feverish land speculation.

The Provisional Government implemented the so-called Plan de Emergencia in an attempt to deal with the unemployment caused by recession and the sudden influx of people into Caracas after the fall of Pérez Jiménez.

Although in many cases this "Plan" did not actually provide work for those who had been employed on the public works projects, it did guarantee these people the income they had received when employed. For obvious reasons, the Plan was to become a source of much difficulty for the Betancourt government during its first year in office.

The new regime was also confronted with the fact that, after almost a decade of dictatorship, there was now a great upsurge of aspiration for change on the part of the depressed and oppressed elements in the society. This was particularly true of the peasantry, who expected the new regime to reinstate the agrarian reform started by the Acción Democrática regime of 1945-48 but suspended by the dictatorship. To meet this demand, the Provisional Government established an Agrarian Reform Commission, with representatives from virtually every interest group concerned with the problem: the Peasants Federation, landlord groups, associations of agronomists and other agricultural experts, the labor movement, organized businessmen, bankers and merchants, the four major political parties, and various government departments and autonomous agencies concerned with agriculture. The Commission made its detailed report, complete with a proposed agrarian reform law, shortly after the Betancourt regime assumed office. [59]

The economic crisis and new demands made upon the Provisional Government provoked a fiscal crisis. The government needed to increase its revenues. There was also widespread demand for a change in the "50-50" formula in the oil industry, which had been established more than a decade before by the Acción Democrática regime. Some Middle Eastern countries had gone beyond that formula by 1958.

The response of the government to these pressures

44

took the form of new tax legislation in January 1959. Income taxes in particular were increased; for instance, the petroleum companies were to pay 60% of their gross profit from Venezuelan oil. As a matter of fact, the new legislation reserved a somewhat larger percentage than this from the revenues of Venezuela's petroleum industry.

Economic difficulties may have contributed to the political instability of the Provisional Government. Two major military coups were attempted against the new regime, in July and in September 1958. Although these mutinies, one of which was led by the Minister of Defense of the provisional regime, caused temporary crises, they were put down within a few hours. The fact that they were met not only by loyal armed forces but by virtually universal resistance from the populace vividly evidenced the widespread desire for a return to constitutional government. General strikes declared by the new Comité Sindical Unitario were backed by most employers, who expressed their solidarity with the Provisional Government.

The Provisional Government and the political leaders outside the administration devoted much time and attention to organizing the elections to choose a constitutional government. As first steps in this direction, exiles were repatriated, all political prisoners of the Pérez Jiménez regime were freed, and the political parties were reorganized.

It soon became clear that the principal political forces in Venezuela were still represented by Acción Democrática, Copei, Unión Republicana Democrática, and the Partido Comunista de Venezuela. However, the relative strength of these four parties was by no means clear until the elections of December 1958.

Because all political parties were in disarray when the dictatorship fell, all their leaders engaged in intensive activity to reorganize local party units throughout the country. The three larger parties held national conventions or conferences to marshal their national leadership and plan for the forthcoming election.

The leaders of Acción Democrática, Copei, and the URD constituted an informal political junta. They met frequently and attempted to maintain a solid civilian front vis-à-vis the military, and to work out plans for the election and other major issues facing the country. For some months the three parties held hopes of uniting on a single candidate for the presidency. However, none of the parties was willing to let a leader of any other become the unity candidate. When this became obvious, the party leaders attempted to agree upon a non-party nominee, again without success, whereupon unity attempts were abandoned and each major party named its own candidate. Acción Democrática quite predictably chose Rómulo Betancourt, although some younger party leaders opposed his selection. Equally predictably, Copei decided to run Rafael Caldera. For its part, Unión Republicana Democrática threw its support behind the aspirations of Admiral Wolfgang Larrazábal, first President of the Provisional Government. He also won the endorsement of the Communists.

Shortly before the election of December 7, the three candidates met in Punto Fijo and entered into what came to be known as "the Pact of Punto Fijo." It was agreed that no matter which of the three won, the other two would recognize his victory; and that whoever won would form a government composed of members of all three parties: Acción Democrática, Copei, and URD. By this accord the candidates hoped to prevent a split in the civilian groups that might provoke a new military coup.

The election was won by Rómulo Betancourt, who received 49 per cent of the total vote, compared with the 70 per cent his party had received in 1948. Acción Democrática also won a majority in the Senate and the Chamber of Deputies. Admiral Larrazábal came in a strong second, carrying Caracas and most of the other cities in the central part of the country; URD won the second largest representation in both houses of Congress, as well as control of the Caracas City Council. Copei made a surprisingly poor third-place showing, with a smaller proportion of votes polled than in the 1947 presidential election; it had the third largest representation in Congress. [60]

The Communists did unexpectedly well in this election, winning one seat in the Senate and six in the Chamber of Deputies. They came out as the second strongest party in the Federal District, and they had won representation in several state legislatures and various city and town councils.

Chapter Two

THE EXPERIMENT WITH VIOLENCE

The Venezuelan Communists emerged after the Pérez
Jiménez dictatorship stronger than ever before.   They
had a degree of respectability they had never previously
attained, and have been unable since to regain.   During
the dictatorship they had gained key posts in newspapers
and other periodicals, which they could now use to good
advantage.   And they shared the glory and the popularity
of all those who had worked in the Junta Patriotica to bring
down a hated regime.

THE COMMUNISTS AND THE
PROVISIONAL GOVERNMENT

Two other factors contributed to Communist strength
during the period of the Provisional Government.   One
was their apparent unity.   A single Communist Party
emerged from the dictatorship, led by the Machado Brothers and other leaders of the old Red party.   The party's
principal trade union leaders in 1958 included Cruz Villegas, a former leader of the Partido Revolucionario
Proletario (Comunista), who had been readmitted to the
Partido Comunista de Venezuela sometime before the fall
of the dictatorship; Rodolfo Quintero, also a former Black
Communist and probably the most important trade union
strategist in the Communist camp, who represented the
Communists in the Conité Sindical Unitario; and several

younger Red trade unionists, such as Eloy Torres. Some followers of Juan Bautista Fuenmayor had also been re-admitted to the Party, although Fuenmayor himself had retired from political activity.

Even more important to the strength of the Communist position during the Provisional Government of 1958 was the attitude of the other political parties. There was a widespread conviction among leaders of Acción Democrática, Copei, and URD that all civilian political figures had to put up a solid front vis-à-vis the military. It was believed that the violent quarrels among civilian politicians in 1948 had made possible the establishment of the military dictatorship, and that repetition of this had to be prevented at all costs. Hence, the general tendency was to play down any dissidence among civilian elements, and it was reflected in the attitude of other political party leaders toward the Communists. Even when the Communists, especially from their vantage points in the press, leveled their sometimes harsh attacks at leaders of other parties, their abuse went largely unanswered.

Thus, although the Communists were asked by the other parties not to take part in the informal junta of party leaders which operated during the Provisional Government, they were nonetheless frequently consulted by leaders of the other parties, and during these months they were virtually immune from open criticism. They found themselves recognized for the first time as a force in Venezuelan politics, treated more or less as equals by the leaders of the other political parties.

This situation was reflected particularly in the labor movement. With the fall of the dictatorship, steps were taken to rebuild the shattered trade unions, and ultimately to reconstitute the Confederación de Trabajadores de Venezuela. To this end, a Comité Sindical Unitario was established, consisting of union leaders from all four parties, that is, Acción Democrática, Copei, URD, and the Communists.

The Comité Sindical Unitario worked to bring together into single organizations the various small unions which each party group had continued to control during the dictatorship. Existing union groups were merged into a single organization, by industry or trade in each locality.

In addition, the Comité Sindical Unitario established a provisional committee to work toward reconstituting the national industrial federations and the state labor federations. All four parties were represented in each provisional group.

Finally, the Comité Sindical Unitario made sure that elections were held in all local unions and that national congresses met formally to reestablish the various federations. Joint slates of the four parties were put up in virtually all the elections which were held throughout 1958, with posts on the tickets allotted in what was presumed to be the respective proportion of each group's supporters.

Under this system, Acción Democrática was the great loser. It still had the support of a majority of the organized workers, and could have won control of a substantial majority of the unions in a straight contest. However, it was given a majority of posts on only a few trade union states.

The other three parties all profited at AD's expense. Undoubtedly Copei and URD, which in fact had relatively little backing among unionists, gained more than the Communists. But Communists, too, were certainly more numerous among the emerging trade union leadership in 1958 than their support within the unions' rank and file would have justified.

The Communists also made modest gains in one other type of organization, and important advances in several others. The Communist showing was least spectacular in the peasant unions. Although the peasant movement was considered part of the general labor movement, the revived peasant organizations were still overwhelmingly AD in sentiment, and the division of union posts among the four parties was carried out a good deal less thoroughly in that sector than in the urban labor movement.

In contrast, among professional organizations the Communists did make significant headway. In these groups—doctors, lawyers, journalists, teachers, etc. — elections were also generally held on a four-party unity basis, and the Communists obtained representation among the executives of groups in which they had formerly had little or no influence. Their showing among journalists and teachers was particularly good.

The Communists also made headway in gaining public administrative posts. Although Unión Republicana Democrática was probably the closest party to Admiral Wolfgang Larrazábal while he headed the Provisional Government, and therefore got the most patronage from the regime, the Communists were not far behind. They won important positions in the Ministry of Education, the Plan de Emergencia, and other government agencies.

Finally, the Communists made substantial headway among the slum dwellers in the hills around Caracas, and in leading their new organizations. Many new "barrios" or slum communities were first set up in the hill areas during the period of the Provisional Government, when private or government lands were invaded for the construction of shantytowns.

Talton R. Ray, in an unpublished manuscript entitled

51

The Political Life of the Venezuelan Barrios, has described the leading position of the Communists in this
area during the Provisional Government in the following
terms:

> Only by understanding this dispersion of politi-
> cal power among different parties on the munici-
> pal level can one understand how the Communists,
> whose party was numerically very weak, could
> play such a key role in barrio settlement during
> 1958. Because the party enjoyed considerable
> influence in various branches of the Provisional
> Government, Communist leaders were often
> allowed to lead invasions. Had they faced offi-
> cials who were uniformly antagonistic (as they
> would have, for instance, if the present Acción
> Democrática leaders had been dominant), their
> efforts would have been quickly frustrated
> (pp. 45-46).

> As in the case of the democratic leader, the
> Communist maintained support because his
> neighbors liked the way he related to them and
> what he did for the community. He was gener-
> ally a very friendly person and had markedly
> sharp intelligence. He was dynamic, self-
> confident and demanded people's respect.
> That his beliefs became the beliefs of his
> friends was due more to his charismatic
> qualities than to their conviction of the
> validity of his ideology. In his barrio, the
> Communist made good use of his personal
> qualities. He became intimately associated
> with group activities and worked hard for
> the community's welfare. If anything needed
> to be done, people learned that he was the man
> to go to. . . . Having once succeeded, the

neighbors were defiantly proud of their accomplishments and could be molded into little
pockets of resistance against the official order
(p. 79).

During the first two years following the 1958
revolution, PCV leaders were very influential
in many barrios throughout the country. Subsequently . . . this strength has been depleted. . .
(p. 149).

Thus during the Provisional Government period the
Communists had more power, prestige, influence, and
respectability than ever before or since. However, in
retrospect, particularly in view of what happened during
the first years of the Betancourt administration, the Communist leadership was not entirely satisfied with the way
the party had behaved during the Provisional regime.
Jesús Faria, in his report as Secretary General to the
Party's Third Congress in March 1961, insisted that the
party had failed sufficiently to delineate the class groupings which participated in the Provisional Government,
and had not attacked sufficiently "the machinations of the
representatives of the conciliating large bourgeoisie"
who were part of the regime. He added that "the mali-
cious action of these sectors within the provisional government later facilitated the triumph of Betancourt and
his policy of surrender to imperialism."[1]

However, one can doubt whether a more militantly
critical policy by the Communist Party toward the Provisional Government would have served party interests
better. It is dubious whether the Communists would have
been able to penetrate government employment, the labor
movement, and even the "barrios" so effectively had
they been highly critical of the regime.

Toward the end of the Provisional Government, the Communist Party faced a difficult decision regarding whom to support in the presidential election campaign. Jesús Faria summed up this problem thus: "It was evident that we could not carry on an electoral campaign either for Caldera or for Betancourt, both of whom had a recognized anti-Communist position. We had to choose between a candidate of our own, or support for Larrazábal. We decided to vote for Larrazábal. We were seeking to facilitate the formation of a government of unity, to defeat the candidacy of Betancourt, which appeared from the first moment to be what was most dangerous for the democratic development of the country. The facts have more than proved the accuracy of our observations."[2]

THE COMMUNISTS AND THE
BETANCOURT REGIME

Certainly Rómulo Betancourt was the last candidate the Communists wanted to win. He was the only one of the three nominees to attack them publicly during the campaign. In his inaugural address he made it clear he wanted no part of them in his government—although the other three parties were represented at the beginning—but he assured them freedom to operate so long as they continued to work within the democratic constitutional system.

At that particular time, this was a politically brave statement for Betancourt to make, and it aroused wide comment. The Communists were at the height of their respectability and power. Communists edited the principal newspapers of the supposedly conservative Capriles chain and PCV members were influential in other newspapers as well; their position in radio and television was important; they were the second force in the organized labor movement; they had close relations with Admiral

Larrazábal, who presumably wielded considerable influence in the military. Furthermore, many of the younger members of Betancourt's own party, Acción Democrática, wanted an alliance with the Communists, and were severely critical of ideological opposition to them.

Even before Betancourt took office, however, the Communist Party had openly opposed the new regime. At a Plenum of the Central Committee in January 1959, the Communists spelled out their position: any government headed by Betancourt in which they were not included would be the target of their ire and opposition. A statement of this Plenum read in part as follows:[3]

> We do not wish to be spokesmen for gloomy predictions, but we affirm that if there is not formed a government of that type—of national unity—the political situation will be complicated in a dangerous manner. According to our criterion, the government of Betancourt if it is faced from its inception with the open opposition of any one of the parties that form the front of unity, will increase the weakness and instability which are implicit in the form in which it obtained its electoral victory and in the factors which worked against the candidacy of Betancourt.

The statement of the January 1959 Plenum of the PCV then set forth what it conceived to be the alternative before the President-elect:[4]

> It is necessary to study objectively the perspectives of the present situation. The constitutional government can orient itself along one of two paths:

FIRST: that of formation of a government
disposed to apply a policy of conciliation, of
advances and retreats, of concessions to
reactionary civil and military, national and
foreign sectors. This policy would condemn
the nation to manifest instability, to popular
discontent, to mass struggles to impose a
really democratic and nationalist leadership.
Our Party would combat with firmness, without any kind of fear and with the greatest
political independence, all concessions, all
vacillations of this nature which might develop.
Favoring such vacillation are elements such
as the well-known tendency for maneuvering
and the policy of conciliation of Betancourt,
the fact that the other parties have not yet
been consulted on the future government, the
rumors of a possible amnesty for military
and civilians guilty of coups d'etat, the economic power and the strong political positions
of the foreign monopolies.

SECOND: the path of formation of a government of national union which, with the support
of the progressive political parties and of all
advanced elements which exist in Venezuela,
of institutionalist-minded and patriotic military,
of independent progressive civilians, will apply
the program announced during the election
campaign. This is the path which can lead our
country to its total political and economic independence. In this form the elements of
instability can be neutralized. In this form
that government may count on the full support
of our Party.

Betancourt was already committed by the Pact of

Punto Fijo to include the three major parties in his administration, was then negotiating with them about the distribution of portfolios, and in fact did form a cabinet in which Copei and URD had three members apiece and his own AD party only two. The Communist statement predicated support only to a "national union" government, presumably in which the PCV had a part, or at least considerable influence. It was clear, however, that Betancourt had no intention of forming that kind of administration, and so the Communists announced their opposition even before he took office.

The PCV responded promptly to Betancourt's announcement in his inaugural speech that he would allow no Communists in his administration. The Political Bureau of the Party issued a statement on the day of the inauguration which appeared in the newspaper El Nacional the following day, February 14, 1959; it read in part:

With regard to the anti-Communist aggression contained in the Message directed by President Betancourt to the nation today, the Communist Party declares the following:

1. The interpretation which President Betancourt gives of the aims and philosophy of the Communist Party does not conform to the truth. The President attributes stupidities to us and then refutes them. This is a worn-out technique.

2. The enemies of democracy are not to be found in our ranks. They have never been in our midst. The source which nourishes 'coup d'etatism' is the great foreign monopolies which have always generated dictatorships for the benefit of their own shady interests and privileges, both economic and political.

57

3.   The whole Venezuelan people is witness of how the Communists have always been in the most dangerous posts, exactly for the purpose of winning democracy and then maintaining and consolidating it. Our Party has fought loyally and with firmness for the victory of a constitutional regime.

4.   It is grossly ironic that the first act of the constitutional president is an aggression against those of us who have fought for the constitutional regime. . . .

5.   This anti-unity, opportunist position, lacking all valor since it takes advantage of our inability to reply to it, does not conform to any Venezuelan motive, but has as its objective the courting of favor in ruling circles and those of the North American monopolistic consortiums, which have no place in our internal affairs and our sovereignty as an independent country.

6.   Nor does it conform with the need, recognized by all political leaders, of fortifying national unity in the face of evident menaces against the stability of the legal regime.

7.   Nor are we sure either that President Betancourt is authorized to attack us in the name of the URD, Copei parties or even of his own AD party. We say this because until today we have not been attacked—since January 23—[*] by the leaders of those parties. . . .

---

[*]The date of the overthrow of Pérez Jiménez.

8.   Finally, the Political Bureau of the Communist Party points out the misfortune which might
result from a government that begins by break-
ing the unity achieved in the long struggles of
our people, weakening the front of resistance
against coup d'etatism. The anti-Communist
aggression has been and will be dangerous for
the stability of a constitutional government.

FIRST PCV MOVES AGAINST
BETANCOURT REGIME

Hence, from the outset of the Betancourt regime,
relations between it and the Partido Comunista de Venezuela were poor. The first open break came in August
1959 when the President moved to end the Plan de
Emergencia established by the Larrazábal government
the year before. Betancourt announced his intention to
discontinue payments under the Plan to those who were
not in fact employed, and to establish in place of the
Plan a modest program of public works.

The beneficiaries of the Plan de Emergencia, pro-
testing these measures held a demonstration, which
broke up in a riot. Several people were killed and
wounded in clashes with police and soldiers. Minister
of Interior Luis Dubuc, a member of Acción Democrática, publicly blamed the Communists for the demonstration and the violence resulting from it, charging that
they had organized both the meeting and the assault on
the security forces. This was the first open attack by
a high official of the coalition government upon the Communist Party, but leaders of the other parties in the
coalition soon supported the charges made by Dubuc.

This was merely a preliminary skirmish; the Communists had not yet launched an all-out attack on the

constitutional government, as indicated in a declaration by Jesús Faria, Secretary General of the PCV, which appeared in <u>El Nacional</u> on April 26, 1960. Replying to certain attacks on the Communists by leaders of Copei, Faria said in part: "We, in contrast, unite with Copei in the defense of the constitutional regime. So long as Copei is disposed to continue fighting for democratic legality, there still exists this link, which unites it with the Communist Party. This was true yesterday, and is so today. Thus it will continue to be insofar as we are concerned. . . ."

In November 1960 a much more serious incident was triggered by a strike of the bank clerks' union, a dissident leftist group that had broken away from Acción Democrática earlier in the year and one of the few unions controlled by Movimiento de Izquierda Revolucionaria (MIR). The MIR and PCV members of the Executive Committee of the reconstituted Confederación de Trabajadores de Venezuela issued a call for both a general strike and a "popular rebellion" against the Betancourt administration. In the ensuing disturbances, 19 people were killed and 265 hurt, 37 cars were burned, 4 police stations were assaulted, and 4 police posts were set afire. [5]

This first call for violent action against the government meant a virtual declaration of war between the MIR-PCV coalition in the labor movement and those union leaders associated with the parties then in the government, AD and Copei. Unionists affiliated with the Unión Republicana Democrática, which had left the government about the time of the strike and rebellion, took an equivocal position. As a result of the flareup, the AD-Copei majority in the executive of the Confederación "suspended' the MIR and PCV members of that body.

During 1961 virtually all the country's unions held regularly scheduled elections. In almost every case AD-Copei and MIR-PCV slates faced each other. The results were a triumph for the government parties. About 75% of the elections were won by the AD-Copei coalition, and probably two-thirds of the country's unions were won by AD alone. Of the remaining 25%, the PCV accounted for 15-20% and the MIR for the remainder. The elections were a fair sampling of the relative strength of each party within the labor movement. They demonstrated that as of 1961, about a year before the beginning of serious violence, the Communists controlled 15-20% of the organized labor movement, and with their allies dominated a quarter of it.

After the events of November 1960, the Betancourt government began to curtail the activities of the PCV and the MIR. Some constitutional rights were suspended by a decree which Congress subsequently ratified. The government temporarily suspended the Communist Party's daily newspaper, Tribuna Popular, and police raided some headquarters of both the extremist parties, although none were actually closed at this time. Under the suspension of constitutional guarantees, no public demonstration could be held out of doors without police permission.

In spite of these restrictions, the Partido Comunista de Venezuela was able to hold its Third Congress in Caracas in March 1961. There, Secretary General Jesús Faria stated the position of the party toward the Betancourt administration and the existing democratic constitutional regime in the following terms:[6]

> The Communist Party understands by constitutionality the result of a whole process of elections to form the different powers of government: National Congress, Legislative Assemblies,

Councils and President of the Republic; furthermore, respect for the constitution elaborated
by the representatives of the people.

In our country, both President Betancourt and
his Ministers and counselors understand by constitutionality the presence in Miraflores of the
president elected in 1958 until 1964, even though
governing without guarantees, even though that
government has massacred the helpless populace,
violated thousands of homes, carried off to prison
thousands of innocent citizens.

These people understand a constitutionality without the constitution. Thus, President Betancourt
suspended the constitution elaborated by Congress
a few hours after it was promulgated. Like
governors of colonies, Betancourt acts above the
other powers of government, and when people
protest this arbitrariness, he then shouts and
accuses those who oppose him of violating the
constitution.

Our Party understands constitutionality as giving
expression to the popular will by defeating imperialism and the other enemies of the people.

Our country completely lacks economic independence; here democracy does not exist but
rather dictatorship of the large pro-imperialist
bourgeoisie which deprives the people of en-
joyment of the freedoms established in the constitution of 1960. And without an authentic
democracy it is much more difficult to defeat
the enemies of the people. For that reason,
to speak of constitutionality and suspend guarantees
without justified motive is to mislead the people,

to destroy their rights. This monopoly of the
government by the Betancourt-Copei group, for
the benefit of the foreign monopolies and the large
bourgeoisie, has not given and cannot give any
benefits to the people; it will produce nothing
good for the country.

The constitutionality which Betancourt-Copei
preach is nothing but the right and the possibility
for the bourgeoisie and imperialism to continue
oppressing our people and exploiting Venezuela,
to sustain the feudal regime in the countryside.

Between the inauguration of Betancourt in February
1959 and the Communist Party's Third Congress in March
1961, the attitude of the Communists had thus become increasingly hostile to the administration. At the XXI
Plenum of the PCV's Central Committee in November
1959, the party had contented itself with adopting "the
task of struggle for a change in the official policy which
would identify it with the progressive and democratic
demands of the Nation, indicating that the policy of the
Government of Coalition would lead to a regrouping of
reactionary forces, by augmenting the divorce between
the people and the government, by favoring the interests
of the anti-national sector of the bourgeoisie and the
North American monopolies and by aggravating the priva-
tions of the popular masses."[7]

However, by the time of the Third Congress the Communists were no longer talking in terms of trying to get
the existing government to change its attitude and policies.
Jesús Faria, in addressing the Congress, noted that
"the last possibility of an understanding to return to the
spirit of the 23rd of January which was opened by the

attempt of 'Los Proceres'* was ended in a stupid manner by the initiative of the President of the Republic."[8]

The hardening of the Communist line was reflected in the resolution of the XXV Plenum of the Party's Central Committee, meeting in October 1960, which proclaimed: [9]

> The salvation of the country is not a simple change of Ministers or a formula to modify the coalition.
>
> A policy identified with the people can be realized only by a government in which the principal role is played by the progressive and popular forces and classes. A policy of national independence and sovereignty can be pushed only by a patriotic and democratic government. Such is the great experience of the Venezuela of the 23rd of January. Such policies have been alien to the governments which have come since that date. Such a lesson must serve to educate the masses in the idea of political power. It will not be possible to think of solutions beneficial for them and for the Nation without their active participation determining the direction the Government will follow.

---

*This is a reference to the attempt on President Betancourt's life, engineered by President Rafael Leónidas Trujillo of the Dominican Republic in June 1960, which took place on the Avenida Los Proceres in Caracas. Although suffering from painful wounds, President Betancourt went on radio and television the evening of the day on which the attempt was made, to make an appeal for national unity in the struggle for democracy.

In this resolution there was no further talk of trying to change the policy of the Betancourt government. Emphasis instead was on the need for a new regime. Less than a month later came the call for "popular insurrection" against the regime, during the bank clerks' strike.

But the Communist Party was not yet ready to engage in all-out violence against the Betancourt government. During the summer of 1961, this author traveled widely throughout Venezuela, and talked with numerous party leaders, Communists among them. Although some local Communist chiefs "predicted" at that time the outbreak of a guerrilla struggle and said that the Communist Party would be aligned with the guerrillas, who would represent the "people, " it was evident that no such movement was yet under way. An actual resort to organized violence did not take place until the following year.

That the Communists were still not ready to abandon legal activities was also shown during this period when Gustavo Machado, in the name of the Partido Comunista de Venezuela, brought an accusation against President Betancourt before the Supreme Court of Justice. Machado claimed the President had acted unconstitutionally in ordering the temporary occupation of the headquarters of the Communist newspaper Tribuna Popular and its temporary suspension in November 1960, The PCV leader further demanded that the Court declare Betancourt no longer the constitutional chief executive. The Supreme Court threw out Machado's charges on the grounds that they were not accompanied by the documentary proof appropriate to such serious accusations. [10]

NATURE OF BETANCOURT REGIME

The growing hostility of the Communists toward the Betancourt government was certainly not because it was reactionary. Quite the contrary, the Betancourt administration was in effect a continuation of the AD regime of 1945-48, carrying forward the reforms and development programs initiated then, with modifications that took into account the changes in the national situation during the intervening years.

For one thing, the Betancourt government undertook an extensive agrarian reform program. The report of the Agrarian Reform Commission, which the Provisional Government had appointed, was received by Betancourt soon after he took office, and an Agrarian Reform Law was passed early in 1960.

Elsewhere, the author has described the 1960 Agrarian Reform Law in the following terms:[11]

The Venezuelan agrarian reform was planned as a rounded effort, which would not only serve to bring about a more equitable distribution of wealth and income but would also have the effect of raising significantly the output and productivity of the country's agriculture. . . .

Various institutions were established or adapted to the purposes of the agrarian reform. The program of actual land distribution was placed in the hands of the Instituto Agrario Nacional. Governed by a five man board of directors, in which the Peasants Federation was amply represented, it had a delegate in every state. The IAN decided what land should be expropriated or what government land should be turned over to the peasants in a given state. It negotiated with the landowners and, if necessary, took the expropriation problem to the courts.

Under the guidance of the Instituto Agrario Nacional, to quote President Betancourt's last annual message to Congress, "Sixty thousand peasant families have received their own land with the distribution of about 1,800,000 hectares. Simultaneously with land, they have obtained necessary credit through the Grazing and Agricultural Bank—which in the five years of this government has extended credits for about one billion bolivares, a figure three times greater than that of the previous five-year period—and technical assistance through the creation of 120 agricultural extension agencies."[12]

Of the 1,538,734 hectares of land distributed by the Betancourt administration between 1959 and 1963, some 868,132 hectares was expropriated from private owners. Such expropriation was particularly noticeable in the central states of the republic, Miranda, Aragua, and Carabobo, where the pressure of rural population on the land was most intense. In the southwestern states of Barinas, Portugesa, and Cojedes, much more of the land distributed in the agrarian reform belonged to the government.

The Betancourt regime made a massive effort to bring the benefits of modern civilization to the rural areas. Virtually every town or hamlet in the country had received either a school, a paved main street, a new water supply, a sewerage system, a small clinic, an electrical system, or a combination of these, by the time President Betancourt went out of office.

The government made other important efforts to raise levels of living, especially in the areas of education and health. The number of children and youths attending school rose from approximately one million when Betancourt took office to 1,700,000 at the end of his term. In March 1964 the President reported that over 90% of all children of primary school age were in school. During the five-year period, some 6,500 classrooms had been built by the government, compared with 5,700 during the previous sixty years. [13]

As a result of modifications made in the Venezuelan educational system, the number of technical and other vocational schools, both primary and secondary, was markedly increased. A completely new educational institution, the Instituto Nacional de Cooperación Educativa (INCE), was set up to conduct a variety of apprenticeship programs designed to train the skilled workers needed by the many new industries and other parts of the expanding Venezuelan economy. By the end of the Betancourt regime the INCE had trained some 35,000 workers in less than three years. [14]

The Betancourt government also paid particular attention to labor relations. Collective bargaining was the established procedure for handling relations between workers and employers. At the time of President Betancourt's last message to Congress, some 3,500 collective agreements were in effect in the country, covering more than 400,000 workers. During the five years of his administration there had been 56 strikes, or about one for every 100 contracts signed. [15]

Nationalism, a tenet of the Betancourt administration, was reflected in two different but parallel policies in the economic field. On the one hand, the administration acted to prepare the way for national acquisition of the country's oil industry; on the other, it sought to diversify the national economy so as to make it less dependent on its principal export product, petroleum.

The regime's major measure toward ultimate nationalization of the oil industry was the establishment in January 1961 of the Venezuelan Petroleum Corporation. This government-owned firm was granted the exclusive right to receive any new concessions for exploitation of the nation's petroleum resources. The Corporation was also to be the ultimate beneficiary of existing oil concessions when these expired, as most of them will, in 1984.

The efforts of the Betancourt regime to diversify the national economy took several forms. The Venezuelan Development Corporation, established by the first Acción Democrática government in 1946 but virtually abandoned during the dictatorship, was given vastly larger funds. These it used to make sizable loans to manufacturing firms in a wide range of industries. At the same time, special attention was paid to expanding agriculture. The Agricultural and Grazing Bank made many more loans to farmers, particularly the smaller landholders and the beneficiaries of the agrarian reform, through its greatly augmented resources. The government carried out a large program of irrigation to extend and improve the land under cultivation.

Building the infrastructure of the national economy was a prime focus of the Betancourt government. The new public electrical generating and distribution firm, CADEFE, brought electricity for the first time to hundreds of towns and villages in the interior, and consumption of electricity more than doubled during the Betancourt period. Some 1,500 kilometers of main highway and, even more important, 7,000 kilometers of neighborhood and penetration roads were constructed in rural areas.

All these programs were carried out in an atmosphere as democratic as the opposition of extreme Right and Left would permit. Although some constitutional guarantees were suspended during the latter half of the Betancourt Administration, the major opposition parties—Unión Republicana Democrática after October 1960, and the split-off ARS faction of Acción Democrática after

December 1961—were not interfered with. The press freely criticized the government, as did many speakers on radio and television. Finally, the Betancourt government presided over general elections in December 1963 in which seven candidates for president were listed, even more for many legislative offices.

Thus the Betancourt regime was one of the prime examples in Latin America of nationalist, socially conscious and development-minded democratic government. This was undoubtedly one of the principal reasons for the increasingly violent opposition of the Communist Party, for the Communists were well aware that the success of such a regime was the most formidable block in their own path to power.

PRESSURES WITHIN COMMUNIST
PARTY FOR RESORT TO VIOLENCE

Between 1958 and 1962 there was rising pressure within the Communist ranks for the party to abandon all pretense at constitutional behavior and frankly to follow the violent road to power. This resulted from the changing composition of the rank and file membership and from the pressures created by the example and precept of the Castro regime in Cuba.

Jesús Faria, the Communist Party's Secretary General, is authority for the statement that the party had been reduced to "a thousand members" by the fall of the Pérez Jiménez regime. He adds that "its ranks increased at an accelerated rhythm," but does not indicate exactly how many members it had at the time of his report, in March 1961. [16] Certainly membership by then was many times what it had been at the end of the dictatorship.

This sudden increase in membership was one of the roots of the strife within the Communist Party. All parties—with the possible exception of the Christian Social Copei—were riven by factionalism at the beginning of the Betancourt regime. This was no less true of the Communists, though they concealed it better. Furthermore, dissidence in the Communist ranks tended to grow during the first years of the Betancourt administration.

Ironically, Communist differences of opinion were intensified by a split within Acción Democrática. In April 1960 most of the younger leaders of AD, those who had engaged in their first political activity during the closing years of the Pérez Jiménez dictatorship, broke with Betancourt and the older leaders. They split away to form a new party, Movimiento de Izquierda Revolucionaria, the MIR which we saw in the labor movement in coalition with the PCV.

Several factors contributed to this division in AD ranks. One was a"generation gap." At the fall of the dictatorship, the party in Venezuela was in the hands of youngsters in their twenties, some even younger. They had fought in the underground, many had been jailed, some had been tortured, and virtually all had moved ideologically far to the left of their elders. Upon the return of Betancourt and other exiled leaders of the party, the older generation (still in their forties) tended to move back into control. Although those who had formal posts of leadership when Pérez Jiménez fell remained at least until the August 1959 convention of the party, it was Betancourt and other elder figures who in fact conducted most of the touchy negotiations with other parties and with the government. Betancourt was obviously the great popular leader of the party, and the older generation had by no means forgotten such figures as Raúl Leoni, Gonzalo Barrios, and Luis Beltran Prieto, who had played leading parts in the 1945-48 Acción Democrática regime.

Some of the younger leaders undoubtedly resented the return to power of those who they argued, had "lived comfortably in exile" while the younger generation fought Pérez Jiménez on the spot. But serious ideological differences between the two groups also contributed to the resentment. The older leaders had a well defined philosophy of democratic national revolution, which they had first applied in 1945-48 and were anxious to reinstate a decade later. This philosophy was somewhat pragmatic, made no pretensions of answering all the problems of human existence, but did stress the importance of seeking a solution to Venezuelan difficulties that was appropriate to Venezuelan circumstances. Their philosophy also emphasized the goal of political democracy as a means of resolving national economic, social, and political problems.

The young dissidents, on the other hand, proclaimed themselves Marxist-Leninists. They felt that the older leaders lacked a Weltanschaung, a consistent method of analyzing social, economic, and even political problems, such as they believed Marxism-Leninism provided. Furthermore, they were impatient with the political maneuvering so essential to party survival in the unstable political situation following the fall of Pérez Jiménez.

The extremism of the younger generation was romantic. If they bridled at the discipline Acción Democrática sought to apply to them, they were equally contemptuous of the much more rigid discipline of the Communist Party. They wanted action above all. And once the Betancourt Administration was in power, they grew increasingly restless at what they conceived to be the slowness of the government and Congress in carrying out sweeping changes.

The younger element which formed MIR were what we have elsewhere labeled Jacobin Leftists. They were xenophobic nationalists, passionately anti-American in

72

particular (with considerable justification, considering the support the Eisenhower Administration had given the Pérez Jiménez regime). They advocated violent change in the social structure, regardless of the costs in human terms. They were increasingly disdainful of democracy and inclined to regard it as merely a system designed to protect the status quo.

Perhaps the extremism of the MIRistas was intensified by the fact that they found little response to their ideas among the lower-class elements within Acción Democrática. The great majority of the labor leaders (and their followers), and virtually the whole AD peasant movement, repudiated them. Thus, although the MIR group thought of themselves as paladins of the oppressed in Venezuelan society, they found that both the real leaders of the oppressed and the rank and file wanted nothing to do with them. This response intensified the left-wingers' conviction that only the most violent methods, which would destroy not only the country's social structure but also its labor and peasant movements, could "save" the people, who didn't want to be saved.

The split within Acción Democrática tended to intensify a somewhat similar division already existing within the Communist Party. With the end of the Pérez Jiménez dictatorship, the Communist Party recruited large numbers of very young members, particularly in the universities. As a force in student politics, it was second only to the left-wing AD group which in 1960 became the MIR. These younger Communists, although they were under much stricter discipline and much more systematically indoctrinated in the party line than their confreres in Acción Democrática, possessed much the same restlessness and desire for action as those who established the MIR.

The AD dissidents of the Movimiento de Izquierda Revolucionaria and the Communists were forced by the political circumstances of the moment into much closer association than they had formerly shared. In the universities they formed a solid bloc that was able to have things virtually its own way in that field for several years. Within the unions, as we have seen, they were soon forced into alliance against the much stronger Acción Democrática and its Copei allies, in union elections which took place throughout much of 1961. In Congress, likewise, the MIR and Communist deputies joined in relentlessly attacking the government upon virtually every issue.

The AD split, therefore, tended increasingly to ''contaminate'' the younger Communists with the attitudes of the MIRistas, all the more because the latter saw themselves in a position to the left of the Communist Party. The older Communist leaders probably were too sophisticated to let such claims influence their political actions—especially since the MIR were making no significant inroads on the Communists' considerable trade union support and their scattered peasant following. The younger Communists, however, were more prone to accept the disparaging attitude of the MIRistas toward any party stance that could be taken as a compromise with the existing social, economic, and political system, and more responsive to calls for a frontal onslaught against that system.

Extremist elements in both the Communist Party and the MIR were undoubtedly greatly encouraged and stimulated by the trend of events in Cuba. The commitment of the Castro regime in early 1961 to ''construction of Socialism'' in Marxist-Leninist terms, the formation of a single Marxist-Leninist party by the merger of Castro's personal followers and the Communist Party of Cuba in July of the same year, and the Cuban policy of training guerrillas and aiding them in campaigns of violence

74

against the governments of other Latin American countries, certainly strengthened the hand of extreme leftist groups all over Latin America.

The Castro regime had special reasons of its own for wanting to see the Betancourt regime overthrown by the armed might of the Venezuelan extreme Leftists. For one thing, the social reform and economic development efforts of the Betancourt government were a standing challenge to the continued assertion of the Cuban leadership that only destruction of the old armed forces, total liquidation of the old ruling classes, and installation of a revolutionary dictatorship could bring rapid economic development and social justice to Latin American nations.

Moreover, the leaders of the Castro government felt the Cuban regime would not be safe until a similar regime was established in an important nation on the Latin American mainland. Only this would divert the attention of the United States from Cuba. To this end, Venezuela would be a particularly desirable conquest: because of Venesuela's great oil reserves, the United States would be sure to concern itself with the problems presented by an extremist regime there; and these same resources would give a Fidelista-type government the economic and financial resources to support a successful social and economic program.

Thus, during the first three years of the Betancourt regime the older leadership of the Communist Party was undoubtedly under severe and growing pressure from its younger followers to embark on an armed struggle against the government. The first important indications that this pressure had been successful, and that the Communist leadership was ready to enter into a general campaign of violence against the Betancourt government, appeared early in 1962.

VIOLENCE CAMPAIGN DURING
BETANCOURT ADMINISTRATION

The campaign of the Communist Party and the MIR
to bring about the violent overthrow of the Betancourt
regime began in earnest in February 1962. In a speech
on May 10 of that year, Minister of Interior Carlos Andrés
Pérez, in explaining the decree issued at that time to "suspend" the activities of the two extremist parties, sketched
the beginnings of the violence campaign in the following
terms:[17]

In February of this year 1962 the national press
commenced to echo with a new activity of the
extremist parties, which would seem to be taken
from the pages of history when Venezuela was
divided in feudal holdings in the hands of omnip-
otent caudillos, and it was as if there were no
popular parties functioning on the national stage
to guide the worker and peasant masses in the
achievement of conquests and specific demands.
I refer to the so-called guerrillas. With a
peasantry fully incorporated into the political
life of the nation, the determining factor in the
electoral process giving life to that democratic
regime which in full sovereignty was given to the
Nation on December 7, 1959, with a social and
agrarian reform in full development in the
countryside, this subversion, defeated in the
urban centers and reduced there to criminal
terroristic activity . . . attempted to copy the
armed action valiantly carried out by the Cuban
people against a dictatorship, the victory of
which was deformed and prostituted by those
who today are the despots of the land of the
Apostol Martí.

In Merida, Portuguesa, Yaracuy, Anzoátegui,
Lara, Falcon, Sucre, Miranda, and Carabobo,
these extremist bands appeared. Small in
number, made up essentially of students seduced
by extremist demagogy and the guerrilla roman-
ticism ably exploited at the beginning of the
planned insurrection by the propaganda of the
Fidelista regime.

Pérez noted that nineteen of the guerrillas had been
killed and nine had been wounded. Fifteen students, most
of them from the Central University of Caracas, had been
captured. He describes the fate of some of the student-
guerrillas: "Some of the narratives of those now await-
ing trial by military tribunal are dramatic. Starving,
fleeing from the peasants, robbing chickens and vegetables
from the peasants who refused to sell them at any price. . .
some lost their lives and others poisoned themselves eat-
ing poisonous fruits."

This attempted organization of a guerrilla war in the
countryside was accompanied by the beginning of a sys-
tematic terror campaign in the cities. Carlos Andrés
Pérez, in the same speech, described these activities:

Caracas and the principal cities of the country
received the impact of terrorist activities.
Molotov cocktails, burning of public service
vehicles and private cars, robbing of commercial houses, assassinations of police, and
more than a hundred innocent lives sacrificed
in street riots. All the means to foment panic
in the citizenry have been used irresponsibly
and with premeditation in desperate efforts to
create an atmosphere propitious to the subversive enterprise. High school and university education, that is to say the culture of the

nation, has been the great victim of this undertaking of barbarism which the agents of international Communist subversion have attempted to mount.

In spite of the growing campaign of rural and urban terrorism, Congress agreed, with the administration's approval, to restore full constitutional guarantees late in March 1962. However, during the debate preceding this agreement interesting details on the organization of the campaign of violence were brought to light. The Minister of the Interior showed Congress "bonds" which had been sold "to buy arms for the Revolution," and others which proclaimed "I contributed a half day's wage to overthrow the Betancourt-Copei government." Passages of the Guerrilla Code drawn up by the underground were also read.

The apogee of this first phase of the insurrectional campaign by the two extremist parties against the Betancourt government was reached in two naval and marine corps mutinies, in Carupano, Eastern Venezuela, in May 1962; and in Puerto Cabello, in the central part of the country, the following month. These uprisings were relatively bloody as Venezuelan military coups go. They were suppressed by the Army and the National Guard and by some loyal naval units, backed in both cases by armed civilians loyal to the government. There is no question about the participation of the two extremist parties in the uprisings. In the Carupano revolt of May 4, Eloy Torres, member of the national Political Bureau of the PCV and a leading light of the party among the trade unions, was caught with a group of sailors attempting to escape from the garrison as the revolt collapsed. The Communist daily paper Tribuna Popular, which was still being published in Caracas at the time, defended Torres' participation in the revolt. Tribuna Popular of May 7, 1962 said:

Eloy Torres carried out his duty: if at the beginning of the movement he went immediately to Carupano, manifesting his support of the programmatic bases of the Movement, Eloy did nothing more than fulfill his duty as a revolutionary leader at the side of the people, without taking into account the consequences which such action might bring him. We protest against the detention of deputy Eloy Torres and demand his immediate freedom.

Later, in congressional debate, representatives of both the Communist Party and the MIR acknowledged the participation of their parties in the Carupano revolt.

A month later, when the bitterly fought Puerto Cabello uprising took place, the participation of the two extremist parties was equally evident. Simon Sáez Mérida, Secretary General of the MIR, was among the prisoners captured in Puerto Cabello.

The two extremist parties suffered immediate retribution for participating in and supporting these uprisings. On May 9, 1962, five days after the Carupano affair, President Betancourt issued Decree No. 752, countersigned by all members of his cabinet:

ROMULO BETANCOURT, PRESIDENT OF THE REPUBLIC, in accordance with the attributes conferred by paragraph 1 of article 190 of the National Constitution, in relation with paragraph 2 of 136, in Council of Ministers,

Considering that article 114 of the Constitution establishes for the functioning of political parties the use of democratic methods in the orientation of national politics;

Considering that the fourth day of the present month there began in the city of Carupano an armed rebellion which menaced the continuity of the constitutional order of the Republic and placed in evidence the active participation of the political parties called Partido Comunista and Movimiento de Izquierda Revolucionaria;

Considering that the attitude of the mentioned parties has demonstrated the firm decision to continue developing acts of violence for the purpose of overthrowing the legitimately constituted Government;

Considering that the situation created by the subversive activity of the aforementioned groups keeps in a permanent state of intranquility the citizenry, with loss of lives and property and disturbance of the activities of the country;

Considering that the same groups are using commands and guerrillas militarily to carry out subversion;

Considering that such a situation has obliged the National Government to decree the suspension of constitutional guarantees, and obliges it to take measures necessary to secure order,

Decrees:

Article 1. — That the Communist and Movimiento de Izquierda Revolucionaria parties are suspended in their functioning and all their activities are prohibited.

Article 2. — That the headquarters, archives and other property of the parties referred to in Article 1 of this Decree will be seized.

Article 3. — The Minister of Interior is charged with the execution of the present Decree.

At the same time, the cabinet authorized another measure made possible by a renewed suspension of constitutional guarantees imposed the day of the Carupano mutiny. This decree authorized military courts to try those caught in guerrilla or terrorist activities, whether or not they were members of the armed forces.

In conversations with the writer in the months following the enactment of Decree No. 752, President Betancourt made a distinction between "suspension" of the activities of the extremist parties as provided for in the decree, and "outlawing" of these parties. He based this distinction on at least two points. First, even during a period of suspension of guarantees, the President could not constitutionally prohibit any political party, whereas President Betancourt felt he did have the right to "suspend" the activities of parties. Second, the word "suspend" implied that the action was temporary, and that whoever imposed it could reverse it. He added that if the extremist parties abandoned their resort to violent methods of seizing power, he would be more than happy to restore them to full legality.

During the year and a half remaining in the Betencourt regime, the campaign of violence against the government by the Partido Comunista de Venezuela and the Movimiento de Izquierda Revolucionaria was continuous. Concentrated principally in the urban areas, it took the form of terrorism against the government, against business enterprises (particularly foreign-owned ones), and against individual governmental employees. [18] Although small guerrilla bands were still operating in several parts of the country, and the guerrillas occasionally blew up oil company pipelines and other installations in rural areas, most manpower and attention were focused on Caracas and other major cities.

The two parties soon organized the Frente de Liberación Nacional, a united front political grouping that presumably was to direct the campaign of violence, and the Fuerzas Armandas de Liberación Nacional, which was the military and activist arm of the Frente. Although the Frente consisted mainly of the principal figures in the PCV and MIR including some members of Congress who enjoyed parliamentary immunity until September 1963, it was not composed entirely from these two groups. For example, one man who was a leading figure in the FLN and served for a time as commander in chief of the FALN was Fabricio Ojeda, head of the Junta Patriótica in the last days of the Pérez Jiménez dictatorship and URD member of the Chamber of Deputies (the URD expelled him).

The activity of the FALN was concentrated in Caracas, partly because the Central University of Caracas was a principal headquarters of the insurrectionists. It was protected by a "university autonomy" statute, which provided that the police and military were forbidden to enter universities. Betancourt generally respected this law during most of his term, although he thought it extreme and unrealistic.

The abuses of "university autonomy" during this period were legion. Shots fired from within the University grounds actually killed policemen and passers-by. Large caches of arms, ranging from sidearms to bazookas, were collected on University property. Terrorists were given asylum within the university grounds.

Those operating out of the University headquarters and other centers of extremist activity during this period, carried out a broad campaign of terrorism. Banks were robbed; policemen were shot; a world-famous racing driver and a member of the United States military mission, among others, were kidnapped; warehouses and factories were set on fire; automobiles were exploded in the streets; party headquarters were fired upon; and numerous other acts of violence and sabotage were executed.

The objectives of the terrorist and guerrilla activity during this period were not entirely clear. Despite its widespread and violent nature, it was certainly not sufficient by itself to bring down the Betancourt regime, or even to interfere substantially with either its social reforms or its economic development programs. These activities had nuisance value, but not much more, although, as we shall note, during the months just preceding the December 1963 elections they assumed a somewhat more serious character.

Many civilian leaders and military officers connected with the Betancourt regime were convinced that the immediate objective of the insurrectionists was not to seize power themselves. Rather, it was argued, they were seeking to create such an atmosphere of fear and insecurity that the military chiefs would be goaded into the age-old Venezuelan habit of "saving the country" by ousting the Betancourt government on the grounds that it was incapable of "maintaining order." If their activities could provoke a military coup, it was argued, the PCV and MIR would then have taken the first long step toward their own violent seizure of power. A military government would not enjoy the wide popular support of the constitutional civilian regime. Furthermore, members and even leaders of Acción Democrática and Copei, who were in the government under Betancourt, not to mention the oppositionist URD, would be forced into an alliance with the military underground of the PCV and MIR to fight a new tyranny of the Army. The PCV and MIR leaders, it was said, were sure of their ability to seize and keep the leadership of any such united front.

As it happened, it was in large part this widespread conviction among military men that such was the extremists' objective that prevented their obtaining it. The military leaders were as convinced as, presumably, the PCV and MIR leaders that the Betancourt government was much less vulnerable to overthrow from the Left than a government of the military. They valued the support of loyal AD and Copei peasants and workers in their struggle to track down the rural guerrillas and root out the urban terrorists. Therefore, they would not move against the Betancourt regime and thus convert today's allies into tomorrow's enemies.

As the end of President Betancourt's term approached, terrorist activity mounted. Betancourt was determined not only to complete his constitutional period in office, but to preside over free and honest elections, after which he would turn over his sash to a duly elected successor. The extremists were equally determined to discredit the electoral process by keeping voters away from the polls and creating an atmosphere in which the democratic bona fides of the transfer of power would be open to question.

The most spectacular and shocking accomplishment of the terrorists was their attack on a train full of holiday passengers a few miles from Caracas on September 29, 1963. In this attack five members of the Guardia Nacional and two holiday-seekers were assassinated. It caused violent revulsion among large segments of the population, and demands that the government take more drastic action against the extemists.

As a result of this incident, President Betancourt took a step which he had previously drawn back from. Although the government had been aware for some time that Communist and MIR members of Congress were involved in planning many of the terrorist activities of their followers, Betancourt had arrested none, respecting their parliamentary immunity. After the attack on the train, Betancourt moved against these leaders. His justification, in constitutional terms, was that the Congress of which they were a part had adjourned for the last time and would be replaced in the forthcoming elections. He ordered the arrest of all PCV and MIR senators and deputies; most of them were destined to remain in prison for several years.

THE 1963 ELECTION

The election of December 3, 1963 was the ultimate test of the Betancourt administration, and of the democratic process of social change in Venezuela. The President had long recognized the importance of his handing power to someone who had been democratically chosen to succeed him. His opponents of Left and Right were equally conscious of this.

Seven candidates were in the race: Raúl Leoni, Acción Democrática; Rafael Caldera, Copei; Jóvito Villalba, Unión Republicana Democrática; Arturo Uslar Pietri, an independent; Raúl Rámos Giménez, the dissident group of Acción Democrática; Admiral Wolfgang Larrazábal, Frente Democrático Popular; and Germán Borregales, Movimiento de Acción Nacional, an extreme right-wing opposition group.

The selection of Acción Democrática's candidate proved difficult. As early as December 1961 the issue reft the party's ranks, when a faction headed by Senator

Raúl Rámos Giménez and known popularly as the ARS group split away from Acción Democrática after it became clear that Rámos Giménez would not gain the 1963 presidential nomination.

It remained an open question who the candidate would be. There was considerable feeling within the party that if possible the two government parties, AD and Copei, should support the same nominee in 1963. To this end they held extended negotiations which demonstrated that although Copei might support an AD candidate for the presidency, there were certain Acción Democrática leaders, including Raúl Leoni, whom it would not back.

Leoni had wide support in the ranks of AD, and was undoubtedly number two man in the party. He was considered by many party leaders of the middle and lower ranks to be much more a "party man" than President Betancourt, a factor which made Copei unwilling to support him. Leoni had particularly strong backing from labor and peasant elements within Acción Democrática.

Other important contenders for the nomination were Gonzalo Barrios, the party's leader in the Chamber of Deputies; Dr. Pérez Alfonso, Minister of Mines and Petroleum, who did not want the nomination; and Carlos Andrés Pérez, a member of the "second generation" of AD leaders and considered by many too young for the nomination.

There were some indications that Rómulo Betancourt was anxious to see AD and Copei back the same candidate, and that he therefore did not consider Raúl Leoni the party's strongest nominee. However, the President did not attempt to impose his view on the party, leaving the AD convention free to name the candidate the majority favored. That candidate proved to be Raúl Leoni.

When it became clear that an agreement between AD and Copei on a joint nominee was impossible, Copei named as its own candidate Rafael Caldera, founder and still head of the party, who had served during most of the Betancourt regime as President of the Chamber of Deputies.

The Unión Republicana Democrática, which in many parts of the country was the principal force rallying those elements opposed to Acción Democrática, also decided in 1963 to name a candidate for president, rather than back a nonparty nominee as it had done five years before. Its logical choice was Jóvito Villalba, who had first organized the party in 1946 and was still its leader.

The "dark horse" in this election was Arturo Uslar Pietri. A well known novelist, Uslar Pietri was also a wealthy businessman, head of the country's most important advertising agency. He had been active in politics since the days of President Medina Angarita, in whose regime he had been chief political troubleshooter. In the 1958-63 period he was a senator, elected on the URD ticket, but as an independent. Uslar Pietri held somewhat the same position in 1963 that Admiral Larrazábal had five years earlier. He appealed particularly to those who were tired of, did not like, or did not trust the organized political parties, and also to conservative elements who advocated greater freedom of enterprise than had the Betancourt regime, particularly a policy of granting new concessions to foreign oil firms.

As for Larrazábal, although he had lost much of the popularity he enjoyed in 1958, he decided to make a second try for the presidency. His brother Carlos, also a retired admiral, and Jorge Dager, one of the founders of the MIR who had broken with that party when it took the violent road, had organized a party to support Wolfgang

Larrazábal's aspirations, the Frente Democrático Popular.

Finally, the two real minority candidates were Raúl Rámos Giménez and Germán Borregales. The split of the ARS from Acción Democrática under Rámos Giménez' leadership resulted in the formation of a small party which until after the 1963 election also called itself Acción Democrática, adding "Oposición" to its name to distinguish itself from the government party. During the election campaign, important figures in the Oposición party left it to support the candidacy of Uslar Pietri. Germán Borregales tried to mobilize the right-wing lunatic fringe which still maintained that Betancourt, Acción Democrática, and the government in general were "Communists."

The election was hotly contested. Not only were seven candidates running for president, there were as many lists of candidates for Congress, besides slates for state legislators and municipal councilmen. The walls of Caracas and other big cities, and of the remotest hamlets, were covered with posters for the thousands of candidates. All contending parties campaigned on radio and television. The newspapers gave wide publicity to the various contenders.

The Communists and MIRistas, the FLN and the FALN, did their utmost to prevent the election from taking place, or at least to keep the majority of the people from voting. Terrorism was intensified, despite the arrest of the parliamentary leaders of PCV and MIR. The FALN warned that on the day of election prospective voters would be shot down, and advised voters to stay away from the polls.

The effect of this campaign by the extremists proved exactly the opposite of what they had apparently expected.

The vast majority of the voters seemed anxious to demonstrate their repudiation of the extremists in the election. Over 90% of the registered voters defied the warnings of the FALN.

Even more important, the victorious candidate for president was Raúl Leoni, nominee of President Betancourt's own party, Acción Democrática. Although his vote was only about 33% of the total, in comparison with the 49% Betancourt had received five years before, it was enough in the field of seven candidates to assure his election. In addition, Rafael Caldera, nominee of Copei, which had shared the government with Acción Democrática throughout the Betancourt administration, came in second, receiving about 22% of the vote. He was followed by Jóvito Villalba and Arturo Uslar Pietri, with the other three nominees trailing far behind.

COMMUNIST SWITCH TO GUERRILLA WARFARE

The election of 1963 represented a major defeat for the campaign of violence to which the Partido Comunista de Venezuela had committed itself almost two years before. It definitely demonstrated that the party's line had failed to win significant support from the Venezuelan masses. The majority of the peasantry in particular had proved still loyal to Acción Democrática; the urban workers widely distributed their support among Acción Democrática and other democratic parties.

Furthermore, if the objective of the heavy concentration on urban terrorism between early 1962 and the 1963 election had been to provoke a military coup against the elected government, it had failed miserably. The armed forces had continued to back President Betancourt, intervened not at all in the presidential election, and guaranteed the assumption of office by the victor in that contest.

For several months after the election of December
1963, the impact of the defeat upon the PCV and the MIR
was shattering. The violence which had been so preva-
lent during the preceding months almost completely stopped.
Elaborate preparations were made to protect the inauguration ceremonies of President Raúl Leoni in March 1964,
but they were needless; the extremists made no attempt
to interfere.

But though leaders of the democratic parties held
hopes that this respite signaled the end of the campaign of
violence, their hopes were premature. The halt in terrorism merely meant that the Communist Party, the MIR,
and their allies were taking time to regroup and reorganize
their forces in preparation for a concentrated campaign
of violent action much more vexatious than the urban terrorism of 1962 and 1963—rural guerrilla warfare.

The new direction of the campaign for violent seizure
of power was enunciated at a Plenum of the Central Com-
mittee of the Party in April 1964. The Moscow-oriented
World Marxist Review reported on the decisions of this
Plenum in its issue of October 1964. An article entitled
"The Communist Party of Venezuela and the Present
Situation," attributed to a "Carlos López," described
the full implications of the new line.

After the usual criticisms of their own behavior in
the recent past, the Central Committee laid down a line
of action on various fronts, but concentrated on guerrilla
activities. López sketched the party's new perspective
as follows:

Another event of singular importance was the
creation of the armed forces of national liberation based on the groups which have thus formed
the embryo of the future people's army. For

90

the first time in our country a revolutionary
program combines the idea of the need for
changes with the means by which these changes
can be effected.

What forms of struggle will the future people's
army use? In the opinion of the C.C. meeting,
the main form will be that of the classical
"guerrilla" or partisan warfare in the rural
localities, with all its attributes. The enemy
is particularly vulnerable in the countryside;
here his control is less effective, and hence
it is here that irregulars can operate with
maximum chance of success and with the fewest
losses. The maximum effort will have to be
devoted to developing the movement in the
mountain areas.

At the same time, of course, we must not
neglect the armed struggle in the towns where,
as the experience of revolutionary struggle in
our country shows, the opportunities are good.
Up till now, the activity of the so-called combat tactical units in the main cities has imparted
a specific character to the revolutionary armed
action in Venezuela, distinguishing it from the
liberation struggle in other countries. Still, it
is clear that this will not be the principal form
of struggle.

In view of what happened in the following two or three
years, it is interesting to note some of the aspects of this
new guerrilla tactic that were discussed at length at the
April Plenum. For one thing, it was emphasized that this
was to be a long struggle. It was no longer a problem of
bringing about the immediate downfall of the Leoni government, but rather of building, over the long term, the basis

91

for a new regime. López commented on this as follows: "Having confirmed this line, the meeting clarified some of its aspects. In the first place it noted that we must be prepared spiritually and physically for a long struggle, and must educate all our fighters in this spirit. This will help us to remove the 'desperation' and impatience which in the past led to mistakes."

The meeting also discussed at considerable length the relationship between the guerrilla struggle and other party activities. López reported:

The C.C. meeting carefully examined concepts which regard armed struggle and other forms of mass struggle as mutually exclusive, and came to the conclusion that this was a superficial, scholastic, and not a dialectical approach. The experience of class struggle makes this quite clear. Strikes, the peasants' fight for credits, or protest campaigns against particular measures may begin in the most peaceful manner and end in violence—as a rule imposed by the enemy.

The position of counterposing peaceful to non-peaceful forms could lead to some dangerous and harmful conclusions, viz.,

—that workers or peasants who do not take to arms at our first call are not revolutionaries, have lost their class consciousness, are scared, etc.;

—that revolutions are carried out by the vanguard, by a revolutionary elite, and not by the masses; or that the masses at best will follow the leaders after the accomplishment of a few bold or spectacular exploits;

—ignoring all the variety of factors operating
in society owing to which one and the same class
consists of people at different levels of political
maturity, education and preparedness, and hold-
ing that all members of a class or social stratum
are equally politically conscious;

—failing to take into account that social consciousness is formed in the course of daily struggle and that those who are today in the vanguard
did not acquire their knowledge and experience
overnight; forgetting that one cannot acquire a
high level of political maturity without having one-
self experienced the effect of all or a good part
of the factors of day-to-day life which impel the
worker, the peasant and the intellectual onto the
path of struggle against their 'own' particular
exploiters, and, subsequently, against all the
exploiters of their country.

This decision that guerrilla activity and other forms
of party action were not to be considered mutually exclusive led to the decision "to participate, insofar as this is
possible, in all legal aspects of public life which could en-
able the democratic and revolutionary movement to inflict
defeats—however minor—on the enemy. This implies the
fight for various demands, including demands of a political
nature, such as the present campaign for an amnesty which
is an expression of the broad national feeling and which hits
the enemy in a vulnerable spot."

López summed up this key discussion thus:

In a word, it is essential to utilize a thousand and
one forms of struggle, to employ all the means at
our disposal with a view to the combined effect of

all forms of struggle promoting the main form, namely, armed struggle. At the same time we emphasize that armed struggle, too, must be primarily mass struggle, that it should be understood as the highest expression of mass struggle.

During the next year and a half the Communist Party was fully committed to the task of mounting a major guerrilla war against the Leoni regime. The success of this effort seems to have reached its highest point during the first half of 1965, and to have declined rather precipitously thereafter.

Separate "fronts" or "zones" of guerrilla activity were set up in various parts of the country. The guerrilla groups in those zones were made up principally of university students, dispatched to guerrilla activity by the parties taking part in the military struggle against the government. Most of these were sent by the Partido Comunista de Venezuela and the Movimiento de Izquierda Revolucionaria. However, there is considerable evidence that the Vangardia Progresista Nacionalista, a group that was headed by José Vicente Rangel, Luis Miquilena and Luis Herrera Oropeza and had been expelled from the URD after the 1963 election, also contributed recruits to the guerrilla forces. Representatives of the VPN may also have participated in the leadership of the Frente de Liberación Nacional, the "political arm" of the guerrilla campaign. [19]

The guerrillas sought both to win over as many peasants as they could and to terrorize those who might resist them. Thus, early in 1965 doctors were said to be accompanying some of the guerrilla bands and offering their services to peasants in hamlets temporarily overrun by guerrilla forces. [20] The guerrillas were also reported to be well supplied with money, which they spent

94

for supplies from the peasants or even handed out as open bribes for support. [21]

On the other hand, the guerrillas frequently resorted to terror against the peasants. For example, they captured Rodolfo Romero, local peasant and Acción Democrática leader in Tapatapa, in the state of Falcón. Acción Democrática Congressman Salom Meza described to the Chamber of Deputies how the guerrillas treated Romero:[22]

> Some ten or more persons, armed with submachine guns, captured him in his house, in front of his wife and small children. They read him this execution list. . . . They beat him, they knocked out his teeth with blows, they broke all of his fingers and toes; and afterward, in the door of his house, in front of his wife, they shot him.

By the end of 1964 the Communists appeared well satisfied with the progress of the guerrilla campaign during that year. One internal document of the PCV, summing up the events of 1964 and indicating prospects for the future, had this to say about guerrilla activities:[23]

> Another reason for optimism is the news we receive from the guerrilla zones. In spite of the great mourning caused by the death of the beloved Commander Gabaldon, the Lara-Portuguesa zone has known how to temper its forces and assimilate the blow. At the present time it has effective control over 125 hamlets. There really exists a revolutionary power functioning with the support of the peasant masses. In Falcon, the enemy offensive has not succeeded in liquidating the guerrilla bases. In the East and in the Great Plains, we are proving the incapacity of the present government to defeat the

guerrilla movement of the FALN. In the new
year the movement will grow. Of this there
can be no doubt. If we know how to unite the
action of the FALN with a correct political
tactic in the cities, 1965 can be, without dealing in fantasies, a magnificent year of combat. . . .

A quite well-informed United States newspaperman,
Norman Gall, writing in The New Leader of April 12, 1965,
described the spread of the guerrilla conflict thus:

The fact is, not only in the states of Trujillo and
Falcon but elsewhere in key areas of the country,
the Venezuelan government is now in a virtual
state of war against guerrilla insurgents who are
following a prescribed course of violence and
economic disruption. . . . The apparent aim of
the guerrilla is to divide Venezuela militarily
during an uprising. With that end in view, there
is now a chain of overt or incipient guerrilla
activity from the first Continental outcropping
of the Andean mountain system near Caburo,
about 30 miles from the Caribbean coast, all
the way south to the Colombian frontier. Using
the principal waterways of the region as their
points of contact, the guerrillas in the mountains
are able to coordinate their operations with those
of their urban counterparts, the Unidades Tacticas
de Combate (UTC), who function in a great many
municipalities.

By the middle of 1965 some democratic political
leaders, particularly of the opposition Copei party, were
becoming alarmed that the guerrillas might be able to
establish control over territory in several parts of the
country, and could thus convert the conflict into a real

civil war, instead of the hit-and-run operation it had been originally.[24] However, it is worth noting that President Leoni firmly maintained in conversations with the author in July 1965 that the guerrillas had been unable to establish control over any significant area, and insisted that they had been forced back into virtually uninhabited areas from which they emerged from time to time to waylay or attack police and army units.

While guerrilla activities were going on in the more remote parts of the country, the Communists and their friends were pushing two major campaigns among the democratic leftist opponents of the government: formation of a Frente Nacionalista de la Oposición, and amnesty for those who had been arrested for guerrilla and terrorist activities.

The Frente Nacionalista de Oposición was to be an organization within which the parties committed to the guerrilla campaign could work with the democratic leftist opponents of the regime. The MIR and PCV hoped that Admiral Larrazábal's Frente Democrático Popular, the ARS dissidents from AD, who were by then organized in the Partido Revolucionario Nacionalista, and the elements which had been thrown out of the URD after the 1963 election and had formed the Vanguardia Progresista Nacionalista, could all be included in this new Front, together with the two extremist parties.

However, efforts to establish a Frente Nacionalista de Oposición failed. Acción Democrática Party deputy Carlos Andrés Pérez explained this failure when he noted the conditions which Raúl Rámos Giménez, leader of the Partido Revolucionario Nacionalista, had laid down for its formation: "There are three conditions for the eventual establishment of such a front which are fundamental for us: (a) that the policy of the alliance be based on the organization of the masses and the struggle of the masses as the basic instrument of the Nationalist Popular Movement; (b) that the program orienting the said Front be profoundly nationalist and revolutionary; and (c) that the strategy and tactics of the alliance be homogeneous, uniform and correspond to the sentiment of peace which at the moment characterizes the Venezuelan people. "[25] Obviously, Rámos Giménez and his party were unwilling to be converted into mere puppets and front men for terrorists and guerrilla warriors.

The campaign for amnesty was no more successful. Although even such an alley of Acción Democrática as the famous writer Juan Liscano, urged the government to have "comprehension" for those who had been arrested for violent activities, the regime did not budge on the issue.

COMMUNIST ABANDONMENT OF
GUERRILLA WAR

In spite of the apparent progress of the guerrilla activities led by the PCV and the MIR, there was growing opposition within the ranks of both parties to continuing the violent struggle to overthrow the democratic regime. Leaders within both groups were coming to the conclusion that the cost their parties were paying was incommensurate with the results.

Open opposition to continuing the policy of rural and urban terror originated within the ranks of the Movimiento de Izquierda Revolucionaria. Soon after the 1963 election Domingo Alberto Rangel, General Secretary of the MIR, began writing letters from jail to his fellow party members urging them to cease these activities and to regain the legal status of their party. The more extremist leaders of his party tried to get him to reconsider, but Rangel stuck to his position. As a result, the MIR split and Rangel organized his own national and regional leadership bodies of the party in the middle of 1964.[26]

At the time of the split in the MIR, the Communists prided themselves on their own unity. However, two years later the PCV, obviously divided, was veering in the direction which Domingo Alberto Rangel had already taken.

Several factors doubtless contributed to this change. One appears to have been the fear that control of the guerrilla and terrorist campaign was escaping from PCV leadership. This was the apparent reason for the first open break in the party's ranks, and for the suspension of the leading Communist guerrilla chieftain, Douglas Bravo, from party leadership.

The rift and the suspension culminated a train of events that began at least as early as April 22, 1966. On that day a meeting of guerrilla commanders reorganized the leadership of the Frente de Liberación Nacional and the Fuerzas Armadas de Liberación Nacional. The minutes of the meeting read as follows:[27]

> Having met on the twenty-second of April of nineteen hundred sixty-six, Commanders Douglas Bravo, Pedro Vegas Castejon, Elías Manuit Camero, Gregorio Lunar Márquez, and Fabricio Ojeda agreed to the following:
>
> 1. To ratify the accord of the meeting of the FLN-FALN of the tenth of December of 1965, with regard to the naming of Comrade Fabricio Ojeda as President of the FLN-FALN.
>
> 2. To ratify the legal validity of the Supreme Command of the FALN, designated in June of

1963 and amplified in the Meeting of 10 December of 1965 with Commanders Eugenio Lunar Márquez, Tirso Pinto, Alfredo Maneiro, and Dr. Germán Lairet and those others who were accepted by the organizations FLN-FALN.

3.   In virtue of the fact that some members of that Supreme Command have died or are abroad or in jail, the CE of the FLN designates the following men to exercise the effective command: Commanders Douglas Bravo, as First Commander; Pedro Vegas Castejón, Second Commander; Gregorio Lunar Márquez, Elías Manuit Camero, Tirso Pinto, Alfredo Maneiro and Dr. Germán Lairet.

4.   Both the Presidency of the FLN and the executive command of the FALN will be provisional until the members of these organs are elected by the National Conference of the FLN-FALN, which will be convoked for this purpose.

5.   The President of the FLN convokes this First National Conference for the preparation of which an organizing Commission will be designated in another resolution.

6.   The political organizations which make up the FLN and the Commanders of the Guerrilla Fronts operating in the country will be notified of these resolutions.

7.   This organization will designate delegations to governments and international organizations which extend recognition. Such recognition will be requested.

This action by the guerrilla leaders provoked immediate reaction from the Political Bureau of the Communist Party. The guerrilla chiefs had acted without first getting approval of the Communist leadership, something which the Politburo of the PCV was not ready to accept. Although on April 24, 1966, a letter signed by Douglas Bravo, Pedro Vegas Castejón, and Elías Manuit Camero and approved by Fabricio Ojeda, was sent to the Politburo notifying the leadership of the action taken and arguing that it conformed with recent decisions of the Politburo that the FLN-FALN leadership should be reorganized, the Communist chiefs did not accept this version of events.

On May 18, 1966, by resolution, the Politburo denounced Bravo, and suspended him from membership in the Politburo. Following are excerpts from this resolution:[28]

> Concerning Comrade Douglas Bravo, the previously cited facts demonstrate (a) there has commenced to circulate—outside the regular channels of the organization—a document edited and signed by him, without previous knowledge of the PB, written on typewriters not belonging to the Party and with positions which contradict the line approved in the VII Plenum of the CC; (b) Comrade Douglas Bravo makes known to comrades not members of the CC political documents which are exclusively for members of the CC; (c) Comrade Douglas Bravo behind the backs of the leadership of the Party, has proceeded arbitrarily to form a parallel and objectively divisionist center, usurping the name of the FALN and of the FLN, an act which lacks all legitimacy, since the leadership of the FLN can be designated

only by the parties, sectors, and personalities who make it up, and insofar as the FALN is concerned, the naming of its executive command corresponds to the General Staff and in the last instance to an agreement among the forces which adopted its Constitutional Act; (d) Comrade Douglas Bravo behind the backs of the leadership of the Party and of the regular military orders, has conducted meetings of Commanders and Combatants of District 1, going over the heads of the Commanders of said District.

It is evident that in the conduct of Comrade Douglas Bravo there are erroneous ideological elements, elements which find expression in a militarist attitude, which minimizes the role of the Party within the revolutionary movement. This for one thing. For another, the conduct of Comrade Douglas Bravo leads to a confrontation of the Party and its leadership organs with his personal prestige, which to a large degree our Party has given him. Finally, Comrade Douglas Bravo has confused in a lamentable way the good taste employed in the national leadership for the conduct of internal divergences, with docility. . . .

In consequence, the PB agrees:

. . . .

3. To suspend from his functions as a member of the PB Comrade Douglas Bravo and to pass his case to the CC.

4. The PB does not recognize and categorically condemns the acts of Comrade Douglas Bravo which menace the unity and discipline of the FLN and the FALN. The decision previously taken that the reorganization of the FLN-FALN should

102

be under the direction of the PB and its Military Commission is ratified.

It was the opinion of the leadership of the MIR that this attitude of the Politburo reflected a growing division in the ranks of the PCV. The Secretariat of the MIR Political Commission commented thus on May 4, 1966:[29]

The line of democratic peace is a revisionist line which has caused and will continue to cause damage to the revolutionary movement. It has served as the basis for the PCV to assume new revisionist positions.

This tendency has internal opposition, but it is not expressed in coherent and clear form. We must recognize that our knowledge of the internal problem of the PCV is now less, chiefly because of the strengthening spirit of defense of the Party, and because of the rise of new groups which contend among themselves.

The guerrillas fought the growing trend of the Communist Party to turn against them. Fabricio Ojeda, head of the FLN-FALN, in a letter to Fidel Castro on June 4, 1966, wrote, "A new breach has been opened in our ranks by the disciplinary measures taken by the majority of the Political Bureau of the Communist Party of Venezuela," and added, "In respect to this new problem, I have been informed that the intermediate and basic sectors, including those in the Central Committee itself, have been reacting against the sanction imposed on comrade Douglas."

In analyzing the situation within the Communist Party, Ojeda identified two factions. One, with a majority in the Political Bureau and the Central Committee but "a minority in the base of the Party," took a position "the essence" of which was: "Present developments permit the revolutionary movement to take the initiative on the political front. Nonetheless, the FALN must order the guerrillas and the UTC (Tactical Combat Units) to fall back. It does not mean simply another truce but rather something more profound; it means diverting the form of struggle. That is, a new tactical period begins, which in place of combining all forms of struggle, would suspend guerrilla and UTC operations."

The other position, which Ojeda insisted was "held by a majority of the Party, but with little support from members of the leadership, . . . not only opposes the alteration of plans and the changes of tactics, but . . . presents strong criticisms of the way the revolutionary struggle has been carried out. "[30]

On July 4, 1966 the PCV Secretary of Organization sent to regional, local, and other subordinate branches a document titled, "Synthesis of the Opinions Sent for Consideration of the Central Committee." It consisted of a series of statements and criticisms by party leaders, most of them recorded under pseudonyms; a large number of these urged in one form or another a "retreat" from armed action. One of the frankest was under the name of "Julio-Mara-Bolaños," dated November 1965. Its Point II read thus: "Necessity of a retreat of the FALN: to take the initiative in the political field, for which it is necessary that the FALN order a retreat of the guerrillas and the UTC's. This is not a new 'truce' but a change in the forms of struggle: to open a new tactical period in which, in place of using all forms of struggle, guerrilla actions and those of the UTC's be suspended; and political initiatives be given first place. "[31]

Later in 1966 Pompeyo Márquez, Teodoro Petkoff, and Freddy Muñoz, three of the most important underground leaders of the PCV, issued a statement to party members which argued strongly in favor of ending guerrilla and terrorist action. In part it read:[32]

> . . . Consequently, the Party must undertake a retrenchment on the military front and recommend the suspension of armed action in favor of proceeding to a regrouping of its forces and their preparation for a new revolutionary stage which must be qualitatively superior to those existing up to now.

> Until recovery has been attained in a fundamental sense, and until some advance is achieved in the promotion of new forces and the regrouping of nationalist sectors, all operations of the FALN must cease.

> This military retrenchment must be accompanied by a political offensive which will permit us to cover the retrenchment, alleviate the pressures of repression, and recover the political initiative.

By the early months of 1967 the Communist Party had moved much further in its evolution from the use of guerrilla activities and urban terrorism. Thus early in March, when Julio Irabarren Borges, brother of the Foreign Minister, was assassinated by terrorists, Hector Mujica, a member of the party's Central Committee, issued a denunciation of the act, and claimed that the PCV "categorically and unequivocally condemns this method of struggle, since it has nothing to do with either the revolution or the defense of the popular cause. " He also sent condolences to the Foreign Minister. Three fugitive leaders of the Party, Pompeyo Márquez, Guillermo Garcia Ponce, and Teodoro Petkoff, issued a similar statement from their hiding place, in the name of the Party's leadership.

Shortly afterward, when a group of guerrillas, including three Cuban military officers, was caught landing on the Venezuelan coast, the PCV denounced the attempt. It accused the Cuban regime of interfering in Venezuelan internal affairs. [33]

By April 1967 the Communist Party had gone full circle on the issue of violence. According to a report in the Caracas daily El Nacional of April 23, 1967, the Eighth Plenary Session of the Communist Party's Central Committee, just concluded, had decided "to lay aside armed struggle and participate actively in the coming elections." The same meeting confirmed the expulsion from Party ranks of Douglas Bravo, still head of the FALN. This change in the Party line had the backing of 54 of the 75 members of the Central Committee. [34]

COMMUNIST LOSSES DUE TO VIOLENCE

Certainly the main reasons for the PCV's abandoning guerrilla war and urban violence were the grave reverses it had sustained from the failure of these methods to bring the Party to power. Pompeyo Márquez, Teodoro Petkoff, and Freddy Muñoz had well outlined this late in 1966:[35]

In broad outline the situation is the following: the armed struggle has suffered severe blows and has weakened. The revolutionary movement at present is not in a condition to continue frontal and open attacks on its enemies. The armed apparatus of the Party has been severely damaged; a bloody and brutal repression is affecting the ability of the revolutionary movement to organize, unify and mobilize the broad masses and give an adequate riposte to government policy.

106

Due to the continual reverses and blows suffered, and to its own weakness which impedes successful action, the armed struggle, by not taking appropriate measures to safeguard its instruments, could lose the role it has played in the recent past, in which it offered a perspective of revolutionary transformation to the masses. In reality, it is not playing this role at present and its future depends on the measures we take today.

The weak armed operations which do nothing but repeat similar former operations, without attaining progress of true significance:

a) Make political action difficult and impede the regrouping of forces against the Betancourt 'gorillas';

b) Let the Betancourt 'gorilla' clique maintain its alliances;

c) Act as a brake and prevent the rapid decomposition of its broad base;

d) Destroy faith in the correct general strategy of the revolutionary movement, whose basis was set down in the 3rd Congress of the PCV and was later strengthened in the successive plenums of the CC.

If anything, the three Communist leaders understated their case. The fact is that the favorable situation which the PCV had enjoyed at the beginning of the Betancourt administration had been totally destroyed. The PCV was completely isolated from the great masses of the workers and peasants, and also from the intellectuals. Not only

had the PCV abandoned virtually all legal means of bringing the Communist point of view to the people of Venezuela,
but few people wanted anything to do with underground Communist propaganda.

The labor movement dramatically reflected the catastrophe which the unsuccessful resort to violence wrought
upon the PCV. We have noted that at the beginning of the
Betancourt administration the Communists held some of
the top positions in the single central labor organization,
the Confederación de Trabajadores de Venezuela, and
that even after the union elections of 1961, which gave
significant victories to Acción Democrática, they dominated
15-20% of the trade unions.

Now this labor strength was almost wholly lost. In
the early days of the urban terrorist campaign the Communists—collaborating with trade unionists of the MIR, of
the other dissident AD group (the ARS), and of the URD—
incited a split in the Confederación de Trabajadores de
Venezuela. When the writer interviewed a Communist
leader of the new Central Unica de Trabajadores de Venezuela (CUTV) in April 1963, he boasted that some 460
unions were affiliated with the CUTV. At the time some
3,500 unions were registered in the country. Hence, by
their own account, the new group comprised only about
13% of the unions—including few if any from the important
oil, transport, or construction industries—and no significant national union federations.

If one takes into account that far from all unions in
the CUTV were controlled by the PCV and MIR, which
were then instigating the campaign of violence, it becomes
clear that only a year after that campaign began, Communist influence in organized labor had suffered a disastrous
blow. Subsequently, this influence all but disappeared.

The PCV also lost whatever influence it had acquired in the 1958-59 period in the country's professional organizations. This influence had depended in considerable degree on alliances with other parties, and such alliances became impossible once it was clear the Communists were dedicated to the violent road to power.

Yet another severe setback was incurred by the PCV in the slum areas in Caracas and other cities, where in the two years after the fall of Pérez Jiménez it had become one of the largest political groups. This loss in the "barrios" was due directly to the resort to violence.

Talton Ray, in his study of the politics of the barrios, already cited, comments on this:[36]

> . . . the strategy of PCV and MIR did not produce the results for which it had been designed. In fact, as their extremist campaign got under way the influence and prestige of the two parties among the barrio people began to decline noticeably, reaching its low point at the end of 1963, as was clearly reflected by the public response to the December elections.

Ray attributes the decline of Communist influence in the barrios to three factors: "For one, the campaign was based on the assumption that many, or most, rancho dwellers were no longer willing to tolerate the conditions in which they lived." But this was "essentially the perspective of the outside, middle-class observer who projected his own impression of wretchedness and misery into the minds of the barrio people" (p. 192). The Communists were also wrong to think that "the antagonism towards the AD-dominated regime was acute enough to induce large numbers of persons to take up arms against it. There is no doubt that there were many grievances regarding AD's role, but while they caused resentment for the party, they did not prove the whole political mechanism a failure." This was because there were democratic opposition parties to turn to, which offered to do the things the Acción Democrática had not done, whereas "the message of the extreme left, at least as it came through to the public, was almost totally 'anti,' concerned solely with eliminating the evils of the AD (and to a lesser degree, COPEI) government; it gave little assurance to the average man that he would be better off later under its direction" (p. 193).

Furthermore, according to Ray, the people did not believe extremist claims that the AD government were "puppets" of the Yankees, because the oil policy under Minister of Mines and Petroleum Juan Pablo Pérez Alfonso was considered nationalist, and because the AD-controlled unions were able to get many concessions from foreign firms and "were likewise not being pushed around by the foreign firms."

In any case, says Ray, the cry of "imperialism" had "lost much of the sense of urgency it had had before . . ." (p. 195). Through its industrialization program, the Betancourt government made it look "as if Betancourt and his party were able to get the 'imperialists' to do some work for Venezuela, instead of vice versa" (p. 196).

Ray also notes that there was little sympathy for the violence in the barrios. He comments:[37]

> The FALN's urban guerrilla warfare proved to
> be a grave tactical error. Its success in creat-
> ing a climate of uneasiness and, to a lesser ex-
> tent, generating a feeling of hostility toward the
> government's methods of repression was more
> than offset by the mood of revulsion that developed

in the barrios. Terrorist activities struck much too close to home for the families to look on dispassionately at the fate of the victims. Almost all the murdered policemen were barrio residents. In many instances, they were shot to death while walking home from work or sitting in their ranchos at night; families, friends and neighbors were witnesses to the acts. Some of those killed were elderly men who had been working for the force for years before AD came into power and were considered about as politically harmful as traffic cops. When the FALN ambushed a train just outside Caracas in September 1963 and machine-gunned to death four National Guardsmen—all the sons of poor families—the disgust was especially strong because, for a barrio youth, it was a sign of social advancement to launch a career with the National Guard.

Finally, Acción Democrática and the government took positive steps to reduce PCV and MIR influence in the barrio areas during the period of violence. According to Ray, "The Communists and Miristas were squeezed out of their government posts, fired by the Ministry of Education, and generally removed from positions of power. Many of the key organizers of the guerrilla warfare, including three congressmen, were arrested and jailed as the anti-government campaign gathered steam. Deprived of their sources of assistance from the higher echelons of their parties, the barrio leaders were severely handicapped."

With the elimination of the extremist barrio leaders from positions of influence in the public administration, Acción Democrática set up its own barrio organization, in which community development projects of the government were included, and faced the extremists with the dilemma of cooperating or attacking the projects sponsored by the

AD government. Since their own status in the barrio communities had been built on their ability to do things for their neighbors, this was a hard alternative for the Communist barrio leaders. Most chose opposition, and the upshot was the loss of their influence among fellow barrio residents.

In the general political arena, the reverses suffered by the Communists were equally severe. Whereas in 1958-59 almost no leaders of other parties thought it politically advisable to attack the Communists, by 1963 no non-Communist leader would defend either the MIR or the PCV. The Communists could maintain only the most tenuous contacts with even the leaders of other extremist parties which did not engage in terrorism and guerrilla activities. It was not so much fear of government reprisals as of alienating their own followers that made leaders of the other parties completely quarantine the Partido Comunista de Venezuela.

CONCLUSION

Thus the experiment of the Venezuelan Communist Party with the violent road to power was a disaster. The Party, which had reached an unprecedented degree of power, influence, and respectability in the years immediately following the downfall of the Pérez Jiménez regime, had utterly failed in fomenting urban terrorism and rural guerrilla warfare. Its influence in the labor movement, professional organizations, and the barrios had been reduced to an all-time low. Its infiltration into the press, the public service, and other levers of power had been severely curtailed. In the general political field, the party had been isolated and virtually quarantined by all democratic political groups, even the most radical. Finally, the Communists' contacts with the great masses of the people, particularly the workers and peasants who their doctrine claimed held the keys to eventual dominion, had been reduced to an absolute minimum.

This catastrophic experience had brought about the Communists' withdrawal from the campaign of violence by the middle of 1967. Although this volte-face in policy was not carried out without an internal struggle, and although it incurred the wrath of the MIR, the FLN, and the FALN— and of Fidel Castro and the Communist Party of Cuba as well—it was a desperate attempt by the PCV to return to the mainstream of Venezuelan political life.

Chapter Three

THE STRUCTURE, ROLE, AND
ORGANIZATION OF THE PARTY

Like its counterparts in other countries, the Partido Comunista de Venezuela is at least theoretically organized on the basis of "democratic centralism." A pamphlet entitled Introducción a la Política Venezolana, written by Guillermo García Ponce, a member of the PCV Politburo, and published by the Party in January 1961, sets forth "the essential principles of democratic centralism which control the internal life of the PCV" in the following terms (pp. 35-36):

The directing organs of the Party are elected democratically by the members of the Party through their assemblies, conferences, and congresses.

The directive organs render periodic accounts of their work to their electors, the members of the Party.

Decisions are adopted in the Party after an ample democratic discussion, in which all members have the right and duty to participate. Once the discussion has been completed and a decision taken, if there was not unanimity, the minority submits to the majority.

Inferior organs submit to superior organs. The National Congress expresses the wishes of all members of the Party and is the maximum organ of the Party, its supreme political and organizational authority.

The pamphlet also gives a fuller view of the implications of democratic centralism in the PCV, at least insofar as they are expounded to the public. García Ponce lists "the rights and duties of members of the Party" as follows (p. 58):

> To participate in the elaboration of the political line, in the decisions of the Party through discussions in his group and in the press of the Party.

> To elect and be elected to the directing organs of the Party.

> To ask for and receive periodic reports of the work of the directive organs.

> To criticize the errors, defects, and deficiencies in the work of the Party.

> To attend regularly the meetings of his group, pay his dues and participate in the actions of the Party.

García Ponce's discussion of "Discipline in the Party" gives further insight into the democratic centralism of the Venezuelan party (p. 38):

> The discipline of the Party is conscious, voluntary, and deliberate, accepted by all of its members.

The basis of discipline in the Party is the unity
of thought of Communists with regard to the
principles of scientific socialism, of Marxism-
Leninism. The conscious and freely adopted
discipline in the Party is based on a scientific
ideology and a revolutionary, democratic, and
just policy.

Discipline arms the Party to defend itself against
its enemies, to defend the people and the revolution; it is of great utility to the Party, allowing
it to accomplish tasks which for other parties
appear impossible.

On the concept of "criticism and self-criticism"
García Ponce writes (pp. 38-39):

Criticism and self-criticism consist of educat-
ing and improving the Party and its members
through studying the experience of its own
errors, through analysis of the causes of these
errors. Criticism of errors aids the Party and
its members to be better Communists. In the
Party, to discover errors is not a crime. To
correct them in time, and using their experience,
serves to educate the Party. Criticism and self-
criticism form part of the motor forces which
develop the Party and its ranks.

Perhaps the most crucial aspect of the Venezuelan
Communists' democratic centralism is their concept of
party unity. On this key point, García Ponce writes (p. 38),
"The acceptance of the principles of Marxism-Leninism
by each member excludes from the Party all division, all
factionalism. The unity of the Party is sacred. To make
any attempt against it is the gravest of crimes."

FORMAL STRUCTURE OF PARTIDO COMUNISTA DE VENEZUELA

The organizational structure of the PCV is basically geographical, although on the lowest level party groups may be based occupationally rather than geographically. On the top and intermediary levels, special organs direct the activities of party members belonging to trade unions, and to professional, women's, and other outside organizations.

The basic structure of the PCV during the 1958-62 period is set forth by Guillermo García Ponce in the following terms (p. 36):

The Partido Comunista de Venezuela is structured in the following form:

The cell can be a ward, a street, or a block, bringing together members resident in a determined living area, or a workplace cell, grouping together members who work in one enterprise. The leaders of the cell are elected by the Cell Conference or General Assembly of the Cell, which is at the same time the supreme authority of the cell and in which all of its members participate.

The Zone (in the Federal Department) or the Local (in the Interior), which groups together a given number of Cells. The leaders of the Zone or Local (Comité de Radio or Comité Local) are elected by the Local Conference, made up of delegates designated by each Cell, which is at the same time the supreme authority of the Zone or Local.

The Region (the Federal Department or State),

which groups together various zones or Local Committees. The leaders of the Region (Comité Regional) are elected by the Regional Conference, made up of delegates designated in Zone Conferences or Local Conferences. The Regional Conference is the maximum authority of the party in the Region.

The National Congress of the Party, which meets every two years and is composed of delegates designated by the Regional Conferences. It is the maximum political and organizational authority of the Party on a national scale.

The National Congress of the Party designates the Central Committee, directing organization of the Party between one Congress and another. The Central Committee designates from its membership the Political Bureau which directs the daily activity of the Party.

In addition to these steps in the Venezuelan Communist Hierarchy outlined by García Ponce, there is evidence of at least one other level of organization in the 1958-62 period. Various state-wide organizations were brought together in "bureaus." At the end of 1960 there appear to have been Bureaus of the Southeast, of the Central West, of the West, and of the Center. [1]

LIMITATIONS OF DEMOCRATIC CENTRALISM

This theoretical structure, in which the rank and file members participate fully in party decisions, and in which the ideas and opinions of the membership are transmitted up the hierarchical ladder to the top leadership of the party, which itself is democratically if indirectly chosen, has never functioned exactly as described by

Guillermo García Ponce. Undoubtedly two basic reasons prevent fact from squaring with theory: the environment in which the PCV functions has, more often than not, made democratic centralism, as ideally conceived, impossible; and even when this was not so, the top leadership has been anything but punctilious about a strict interpretation of democratic centralism.

In the thirty-seven years between 1931, when the PCV was formally established, and 1968, the year these words are being written, the party was legally constituted only between 1945 and 1950 and between 1958 and the middle of 1962. In addition, it operated more or less free from police interference, although without legal recognition as a political party, during 1936 and half of 1937, between 1941 and 1945, and during 1968. Thus, it has been able to function more or less normally in only sixteen of its thirty-seven years of existence.

Information is available on the disastrous impact of illegality during the Pérez Jiménez regime. In a highly interesting unpublished study of the Communist Party by the Dirección General de Policía in 1963 (which we shall hereafter refer to as Digepol Study), it is reported that at the time of the Fifteenth Session of the Party's Central Committee, in April 1958, "directing nuclei" of the party existed only in the states of Zulia, Lara, Aragua, Miranda, Bolivar, Carabobo, Anzoátegui, and the Federal District. At this time the party organization was reported as "weak" and apparently without formal regional committees in the states of Falcón, Monagas, Sucre, Trujillo, Portuguesa, Táchira, Mérida, Apure, Barinas, Cojedes, Guárico, Nueva Esparta, and Yaracuy, and having no organizations whatever in the federal territories of Delta Amacuro and Amazonas. [2]

Partly as a result of its precarious legal existence,

the PCV by 1967 had held only three national congresses in the previous twenty-one years, in spite of the party rule requiring one every two years. The first was the Unity Congress of November 1946, regarded by the party as its First Congress. In August 1948 a Second Congress was held, and the next one did not take place until March 1961.

The long hiatus between the Second and Third Congresses of the Partido Comunista de Venezuela is explained partly by the fact that the party was illegal between 1950 and 1958. However, this does not explain why no Communist Congress was held between January 1958 and March 1961, particularly when the country's three major parties, Acción Democrática, Copei, and Unión Republicana Democrática all held congresses in 1958, preceding the December election.

In the interims between Congresses, the party leadership has been akin rather to the College of Cardinals than to a democratically chosen party leadership. Vacancies in the top leadership have been filled by surviving members of the leadership, who in turn determine whether or not members of subordinate bodies are still in good standing.

One example of this method of functioning was given by the Fifteenth Plenary Session of the Central Committee, the first one to meet after the fall of the Pérez Jiménez dictatorship. It drew up a list of names of likely candidates for vacancies on the Central Committee, the final decision apparently being left to the Political Bureau. [3] Of course, according to the party rules, such a decision should have been taken only by a Party Congress.

These more or less self-perpetuating higher bodies have often taken decisions of key importance to the life of the Communist Party, decisions impossible of appeal to a party congress. Thus, for instance, in 1951 Juan Bautista Fuenmayor, until then Secretary General of the Party, and others associated with him, were not only expelled from the top leadership but from the Party itself, by a Plenum of the Central Committee. The decision to launch guerrilla warfare at the beginning of 1962, and the decision to call it off in the middle of 1967, were both taken without benefit of a national party congress.

The Digepol Study comments at some length on the tight internal control of the PCV:[4]

Although in theory, the members of the Political Bureau are chosen by the Central Committee the recommendations of the important leaders of the Party appear to be decisive. Before the Second Congress* various recommendations were made for changing top leaders. One of these is written on stationery of the Chamber of Deputies, which indicates that its author is Gustavo Machado or Guillermo García Ponce. It recommends that the members of the Secretariat be augmented to five and that Luis Emiro Arrieta be withdrawn from FEDEPETROL to become part of the Secretariat, where he would dedicate his whole time to Party organization. It is recommended that Eloy Torres be charged with trade union affairs and Alonso (Ojeda) with agrarian affairs. It recommends that, although Martín J. Ramírez has talent and is devoted, he should be removed

---

*Reference here is apparently to the Third Congress of March 1961, rather than to the Second, which had been held thirteen years before.

from the post of Secretary of Finance because
he seems to be converting that Secretaryship
into a treasury of the Party. It is recommended
that Hector Rodriguez Bauza, who was then in
the Communist Youth, replaced him. It is recommended that Eduardo Machado be given the
work of propaganda and press, Guillermo García
Ponce that of education, Pedro Ortega that of the
Regional Committee of the Federal District and
Eduardo Gallegos Mancera that of an international
relations commission in which would participate
Hector Mujica, Carlos Augusto León and another
person. It recommends that Pompeyo Márquez
be charged with the work of the Economic Commission and with the Theoretical Review, Gustavo
Machado with Tribuna Popular and Eduardo
Machado with the intellectuals. . . .

ORGANIZATION OF TOP LEADERSHIP

Whatever the statutes of the Partido Comunista de
Venezuela may proclaim, the most powerful organizations
within its hierarchical structure are the Political Bureau
and its Secretariat. Considerable information is available concerning these groups and other elements in the
top leadership working under their direction in 1961.

At that time there was a five-man Secretariat, headed
by Secretary General Jesús Faria, who was also in charge
of trade union and youth activities. Other members included Pompeyo Márquez, in charge of international relations, propaganda and finances; Gustavo Machado, "special affairs" and education; Alonso Ojeda R. , in control
of agrarian and mass organizations; and Luis Emiro Arrieta, charged with Interior and the Federal District.

The Political Bureau itself consisted of ten members,

in addition, presumably, to Secretary General Faria.
These were Gustavo Machado, Pompeyo Márquez, Eloy
Torres, Luis Emiro Arrieta, Guillermo García Ponce,
Eduardo Machado, Hector Robríguez Bauza, Eduardo
Gallegos, Martín J. Ramírez, and Alonso Ojeda Olachea.

Various specialized organizations under the Secretariat and the Political Bureau were concerned with particular aspects of the party's work. These included a liaison
group with the Party's parliamentary bloc, a National
Organization Commission, a National Commission of
Intellectuals, a National Education Commission, a National Propaganda Commission, and a National Women's
Commission. Other special groups dealt with the party's
units among teachers, doctors, and lawyers. Perhaps
most interesting of all, in view of later developments,
was an unnamed party unit, headed by Douglas Bravo,
which was charged with preparing the Party's paramilitary
organization. [5]

In 1961 the Central Committee of the Partido Comunista de Venezuela consisted of fifty-one full members and
twenty-nine alternate members. Among the full members
were at least two former leaders of the "Black" Communist Party of the 1940's and early 1950's, Rodolfo Quintero and Cruz Villegas. Douglas Bravo, who was to become the Party's principal guerrilla leader, was then a
member of the Central Committee, but not of the Political
Bureau, to which he was apparently co-opted sometime
later. [6]

One of the most important Party organizations was
the National Finance Commission. In 1961 it consisted of
members directly representing the Political Bureau, the
Regional Committee of the Federal District, and the Communist Youth, besides various other party leaders. [7]

Information is available concerning the amounts of money spent by the national headquarters of the Communist Party in three different periods. Between July and December 1953, when the Party was operating underground, it dispensed a total of 42,000 bolivares (about $12,000), of which 19,800 bolivares was for salaries. In March 1960, by contrast, the Communist Party national office spent some 93,611.55 bolivares, 53,835 bolivares for salaries. Finally, in March 1962, when the Party's campaign of violence was already getting under way, the Communist headquarters spent some 24,300 bolivares in the last two weeks of the month, of which 20,075 went for salaries.

Some interesting information is also available on the sources of the national Communist leadership's finances in the period following the fall of the Pérez Jiménez dictatorship. Table 1 indicates the normal sources of funds each month during the last three months of 1959:[8]

Table 1

PCV Headquarters Revenue Sources

Source	Bolivares per month
Ordinary dues	8,000
Congressional Functionaries	2,000
Salaries, Supreme Electoral Council	3,000
National Functionaries (IAN, CEI, etc.)	2,000
Members of Congress	53,400
Commercial profits	1,000
Profits from bookstore and movies	5,000
Propaganda	500
Membership cards	500
Miscellaneous activities of Finance Commission	13,800
	89,200

It is interesting to note that the largest single contribution to the national finances of the PCV at this time came from the salaries of Communist members of Congress. Other Communists who held governmental positions, then apparently patronage at the Party's disposal, were also significant contributors to the Party coffers, turning over a portion of their salaries to the national headquarters. Almost two-thirds of the total income of PCV national headquarters seems to have originated from people who held jobs in one or another segment of the public administration, jobs received as a direct result of the Party's influence.

AUXILIARY AND SUPPORTIVE AGENCIES 1958-62

Juventud Comunista (Communist Youth) and the various Party training schools were the most important of the several organizations, under the general supervision of the Politburo and its Secretariat but ancillary to the Party itself, which the PCV maintained while it operated principally in the open, between the overthrow of the Pérez Jiménez dictatorship in January 1958 and the Party's resort to violence early in 1962.

Unfortunately, relatively little information is available concerning the organization and operation of Juventud Comunista. It is known that just after the overthrow of Pérez Jiménez the Party leadership was afraid of too independent an attitude on the part of the JC. It is also known that Juventud Comunista grew rapidly in the post-dictatorship period, becoming for the first time in Party history a major factor among Venezuelan university students. With the left-wing members of Acción Democrática, who in 1960 had formed Movimiento de Izquierda Revolucionaria, it completely dominated most of the university student organizations. We have indicated that this sudden influx of young people into the JC and the Party itself was of primary importance in pushing the PCV into the disastrous experiment of trying to seize power by force between 1962 and 1966-67.

Insofar as possible, the Juventud Comunista was integrated at all levels with the adult party leadership. It was represented in important functional organizations of the Party, and some of its leaders, including Germán Lairet, were also in the top echelon of the Party.

More is known about the Party's training adjuncts. They ranged from a school for preparing middle- and lower-rank leaders, through courses specialized according to subject matter and audience, to general classes for rank and file members.

The top school of the Party was the so-called Escuela de Cuadros del Comité Central (Cadre School of the Central Committee). During 1960 it ran five courses of thirty-three days each, including such subjects as Historical Materialism, Political Economy, History of the Labor Movement, Party Organization, The Party Line, and Dialectical Materialism. Each regional organization of the Party was supposed to send one or two students for each course, although the total attending the five courses indicates that these quotas were not always met. [9]

The Instituto Ezequiel Zamora, named after a hero of the Federal War of the 1860's, was lower in the educational hierarchy. During 1960 it presented three-day courses for workers in the Federal District and the states of Anzoátegui, Monagas, Aragua, Falcón, Bolivar, and Carabobo. It also offered special courses in economics, two to five days' duration, in the states of Lara, Zulia, Anzoátegui, and Falcón. Finally, it offered "elemental courses" of four to five days in nearly all the states, and more than one such session in half a dozen. [10]

The Digepol Study outlines the educational program of the Party for 1961 as follows:[11]

126

The educational plan of 1961 was designed so that
all members of the Party would take the elemental
course, Introduction to Politics. The plan had
three stages: (1) preparation of instructors; (2)
instruction in the cells; (3) to offer the course to
sympathizers and all new members of the Party.
The first stage was completed in 16 states before June 1961 and would be completed in three
others by the end of June. Meetings of delegates
of the zones would meet to assure that the regional committees were fulfilling the plan. A
special pamphlet, Introducción a la Política,
served as the text for the course in the cells.

The second part of the plan of 1961 was a course on
the political line based on the Third Congress
which would be given by members of the Central Committee and of the National Education Commission.

The third part would consist of the publication
and distribution of Principios* and of the Report
of Jesús Faria (it would be his report to the Third
Congress). The importance of this material is
that it was for study within the Party and for outside distribution in the AD, URD, and MIR parties.

UNDERGROUND AND PARAMILITARY
ORGANIZATION 1958-1962

Although the Communists did not launch an all-out
campaign to overthrow the Betancourt government by
violent action until the early months of 1962, they had

---

*Principios was the Party's so-called "theoretical"journal.

been preparing for some such eventuality for several years. Of course, the Party had been underground during the Pérez Jiménez regime, and there is good indication that it did not completely dissolve its underground organization, including the paramilitary arm, after the fall of the dictatorship.

In the Thirteenth Plenary Session of the Central Committee, held in February 1957, a little less than a year before the ousting of the Pérez Jiménez regime, the efficiency of the Party's underground apparatus had been extensively criticized. It improved during the later months of the year, as the pressure against the dictatorship mounted but as we have noted, Communist organization by early 1958 was confined to a minority of the states.

After the fall of Pérez Jiménez in January 1958, the Communists obviously sought to maintain themselves in a position to return to illegal work, if required by objective circumstances or Party policy. The Digepol Study comments on these preparations:[12]

> . . . When the Party was legal and participated in the Government in 1958, the problems of the APPARATUS were assigned to Napoleon (probably Napoleon Granados), who was linked by later documents with the clandestine apparatus. . . .
> The National Education Committee in collaboration with the Communist Youth of the State of Miranda prepared publicly a mimeographed pamphlet with the title "How to Act Against the Repressive Organs of the Government and How to Struggle by Means of Our Propaganda," which dealt in general terms with clandestine methods. It discusses secret work, legal work, clandestine work of the Party touching the five themes of Guillermo García Ponce used in the cadre school

of the PCV. Its date of publication was 1961
when the Party had commenced to pass into
clandestine operation after the Third Congress.
All of this indicates that the PCV did not completely dissolve its clandestine apparatus when it
became legal.

This Digepol document has extensive information on
specific preparations made by the Party for possible guerrilla warfare during the early years after the fall of Pérez
Jiménez. It notes a list of "rifles, shotguns, machine-
guns, and pistols which the PCV possessed in that period,
as well as an extensive list of aerial maps and special
maps of various regions." Another memorandum of the
Party cited in the Digepol Study discusses the strategic
importance of possible guerrilla operations in the states
of Lara, Mérida, Táchira, and Falcón, "and the possibility of isolating the western region from the rest of the
country and extending operations to the llanos." It also
listed key roads and railroads in the area.

The Digepol Study notes, "There are other documents
with training material prepared locally: (how to construct
bombs, mines, and other explosive contraptions) and local
reprints of Chinese, French, Italian, and other materials
on guerrilla warfare. There is a report of the Minister
of Defense with the title 'Operations Against Irregular
Forces.' "

The Digepol Study indicates that Douglas Bravo was
particularly active in preparing for guerrilla action, under
the direction of the Political Bureau. He submitted to the
Bureau perhaps as early as 1959 a detailed study of preparations in one particular region of the country, whose ex-
act location is not clear.[13]

EFFECT OF VIOLENCE ON
PCV ORGANIZATION

Whatever damage the Pérez Jiménez dictatorship did
to the organizational structure of the PCV, the effect on
the Party apparatus of the resort to violence against the
Betancourt-Leoni government was a good deal more devastating. The party organization was stronger and more
extensive in 1961, just before the outbreak of violence,
than in 1948, at the advent of the dictatorship. Therefore,
the Communists in 1961 had much more to lose in organizational terms than they had had thirteen years earlier.

Several Communist documents indicate the impact the
campaign of violence had on various Party activities. One
of these is a circular from the Political Bureau to all regional organizations of the Party early in 1964, dealing
with the PCV's financial situation. It reflected a crisis
in the party's finances, and predicted an even greater one
to come in 1964. In part, this circular read as follows:[14]

> In the course of '63 there was applied through-
> out the country a dangerous financial policy
> which totally annulled the initiative of our mem-
> bership in this important aspect of our activity,
> and obliged the DN (Dirección Nacional) to under-
> take extraordinary allocations to take care of the
> increased costs of the functioning of our organiza-
> tion. The financial work has been abandoned to
> such a degree that the immense majority of our
> regional groups did not collect even 10% of their
> expenses, and in the whole country only two re-
> gions made contributions of any importance to
> the National Secretary of Finances.
>
> This has created a situation of real gravity,
> which has alarming characteristics if one

analyzes the financial perspectives of the year
now beginning and studies the reports of the regional meetings of December. One cannot see
in the discussions which have been carried on
an objective analysis of the problem, nor does
the activity of our membership show that it
understands the reality of the situation. The
financial campaign of the year's end has produced ridiculous results; the comrades have
not even bothered to provide figures. Nor is
there evident the application of a policy of
austerity which would provide the maximum
benefit from the funds sent by the DN. Exaggerated expenditures for many items are
being made, there is not full-time work by all
of the functionaries.

The picture the Politburo paints for 1964 is even
bleaker than that for 1963. On this subject, the circular
says:

In 1964 the DN will have income much below
that obtained in the last year. Only one of its
sources, that derived from the salaries of the
parliamentarians, will suffer a decline in the
order of 50,000 bolivares per month; the contributions of some members with government
jobs, which provided 10,000 bolivares a month,
will also be reduced to 0 starting on March 2;
many contributions justified by the electoral
year of 1963 will be substantially reduced this
year.

Speaking in numbers, the total income foreseen
by the DN for the whole year will not permit
covering the costs of the Party until the month
of June; that is to say, even if we are exaggeratedly

austere, if measures are not taken which change
the financial criteria of the Party, we shall be
obliged to suspend many activities in the month
of July, because we shall not be in a position to
finance them.

The circular summed up the Party's pressing financial
situation in the following terms:

It is necessary, then, that true emergency measures be taken to convince all members of the Party
that it is necessary to change our financial mentality, that it is necessary to diminish expenses without diminishing activity and carry out work according to plan so that we can be self-sustaining finan-
cially by the middle of this year.

Somewhat later in 1964, at an unspecified date, the
Political Bureau sent out another circular "to all organizations of the Party and the Youth," which indicated that the
financial situation had not improved. The circular announced that "except for the four fundamental regions,"
contributions of the national headquarters to state organizations were immediately reduced by 50%. At the same
time, contributions to the four key regions were frozen at
current levels and future financing from national headquarters "will depend fundamentally on the resources they
themselves are able to contribute."

Moreover, the circular indicated that rank and file
members were seriously delinquent in paying their dues.
It ordered "the Bureaus of the District, Regional, and
Local committees" to take various measures, among
them "a detailed analysis of the payment of ordinary dues
by each member. . . ." It also ordered a cut of unspecified size in the number of functionaries employed by subordinate organizations of the Party. [15]

However, by late 1964 it was not only the finances of the organization that worried the leaders of the PCV. A report taken by government forces from a guerrilla group in the state of Zulia contained a detailed analysis of PCV weaknesses in that state. This report noted in explanation of the Party's difficulties that "the revolutionary movement is experiencing a period of difficulties which have their origin in the repression loosed against it and against the popular movement in general."

The effects of the situation on the Party are spelled out in some detail as follows:[16]

Organizationally we continue as before. We do not act and we do not organize for the new situation. Previously we talked of the change to a new kind of struggle and consequently our organization must suffer some transformations to put us abreast of the new situation. The directing organs must be more agile and effective to be prepared to direct the Party in any situation, to act with autonomy of action within the general line (strategic centralization and tactical decentralization). In a word, they must be adequate for their directive responsibilities, if the war imposes total or partial isolation, in certain stages of the rebirth of the struggle. The base organizations... must equip themselves with sufficient resources to act in similar situations... to investigate, maintain and know how to reestablish links with the masses....

In addition to the inadequate number of cadres, those which we do have possess the following characteristics: few are well located to help the front, the group which they understand best and are best able to develop without excessive waste;

or they are not located in the best situation,
well studied. The aid which they give is not
sufficient, and in other terms we may say that
we lack a cadre policy which takes into account
the situation of the cadres themselves, what
they have and what they lack, their degree of
development and maturity (experience), so as
to make them advance politically and ideologically. There must be opportune and merited
promotions (it is not that those are promoted
who don't deserve it but that this must be well
planned). . . .

Our organization does not manage tasks in their
diversity, but generally develops its work in one
direction only, one sole task; which generally
once it is completed is not taken advantage of. . . .

To await all initiative from the leadership.
This is a generalized custom in the whole
party. . . .

The leadership is also criticized in this memorandum.
It is accused of not being completely informed ''of the
conditions and situations of the region in its diverse aspects. . . .'' Furthermore, the leadership of the Party
in Zulia ''lacks sufficient preparation, agility, autonomy,
etc., in the face of the bad situation.'' Likewise, it is
argued, its work is not planned, and when it is, insufficient attention is paid to following up on how plans are
carried out. Finally, the regional leadership of the Party
in Zulia does not do enough to encourage the activities of
local leaders and rank and file members.

These financial and organizational difficulties of the
PCV while it pursued the violent road to power indicate
some of the damage done by that policy to Party structure

and functioning. They also give some of the probable reasons for the Party leadership's decision to abandon the guerrilla effort.

STATUS OF PCV

The status of the Partido Communista de Venezuela within the general political system has changed from one period to another. It has twice experimented with being a more or less accepted member of the democratic political process—during the 1945-48 Acción Democrática regime, and from 1959 until it began to seek power through force early in 1962. In other periods it has either been underground or has been at best regarded as on the fringes of normal political activity.

Except in the second half of the first decade of their existence, the Venezuelan Communists have never been in the position of recognized spokesmen for a specific economic and social group in the body politic. During the 1936-44 period they were the dominant element in the organized labor movement, but in 1944 they lost this position. In 1958-60 they assumed an important position of leadership—although by no means an exclusive one—in the shanty-town barrios on the hills above Caracas. However, as we have seen, they lost this position also. The Communists have never had much influence among the peasantry, the other oppressed group in society to which they might be expected to appeal. Recent immigrants, another subculture not yet fully integrated into Venezuelan society, have been largely apolitical and the Communists have had little influence among them.

At various times during its existence, the Communist movement in Venezuela has been illegal. During the Gómez and López Contreras administrations, from 1931 to 1941, and during the Pérez Jiménez dictatorship of the 1950's, this was not the Communists' own decision, but that of the military regimes. However, in the years 1962-67, the Communists were again illegal and had to operate largely underground because of their own deliberate decision to resort to violence against a constitutionally elected democratic government.

Except during the López Contreras period, the outlawed status of the Communists weakened them substantially. Under López Contreras, when persecution of the Party was less severe than of other political groups, the Communists were able to consolidate their influence in the labor movement.

During the dictatorship of the 1950's, the Communists were split at least part of the time. The so-called "Black" faction, the Partido Revolucionario Proletario (Comunista), maintained its influence in organized labor and continued to operate legally until shortly before the fall of Pérez Jiménez. The "Red" element, the Partido Comunista de Venezuela, was more severely treated.

However, although their membership was greatly reduced during the dictatorship, the Communists were able to make certain long-range gains. Neither the Reds nor the Blacks were persecuted as severely as was Acción Democrática, which the regime considered its major opponent, with the result that the Communists had a good deal more freedom than AD to disseminate their ideas among students and political prisoners in jails and concentration camps. They also found it easier to carry on their propaganda "in the streets."

These facts and the general conditions of the dictatorship tended to drive the younger people of Acción Democrática and other parties to the extreme Left. Thus, the Communists emerged with a much larger following among youth, particularly university students, than ever before. The belated participation of all elements of the Communist movement in the final struggle against the Pérez Jiménez dictatorship had given the Communists, by January 1958, greater respectability and prestige than they had ever enjoyed before.

But as we have seen, the Communists nearly destroyed their influence and prestige of the 1958-61 period by their urban terrorism and guerrilla warfare in the next four years. As a result, they had reached a low point of power and acceptability when they once again reversed their policy in 1966-67.

The periods of legality and constitutional functioning of the PCV have never been long enough to present it with the problem faced by some other non-governmental Communist parties, even in Latin America. They have never seriously compromised with the "bourgeois" democratic system for any length of time, they have never become entrenched in this system, nor shared its power and influence long enough, to be tempted to accept its rules and postpone more or less indefinitely their aspirations to power. Peculiar circumstances, which we have described at length in the historical part of this monograph, prevented the Party from making such a compromise when it might have done so, between 1958 and 1962.

MEMBERSHIP AND LEADERSHIP IN THE PCV

The size of the Venezuelan Communist Party's membership has varied widely during its history. Table 2 gives estimates over a 20-year period.

The figures for Communist Party membership are taken, with one exception, from the annual publication of the Bureau of Intelligence Research of the United States

Table 2

Membership of Venezuelan
Communist Movement

Year	Membership	% of Population
1947	20,000	0.5
1952	10,000	0.2
1957	1,000	0.016
1958	9,000	0.16
1961	40,000	0.57
1967	10,000	0.12

Department of State entitled World Strength of the Communist Party Organizations. The exception is the year 1957,
where the figure given is the one PCV Secretary General
Jesús Faria presented to the Party's Third Congress for
the end of the Pérez Jiménez dictatorship.

From the author's personal contacts with the Communist Party of Venezuela over the years, he is inclined to
think that the figures for 1947 and 1967 are somewhat
larger than the real membership of the Party on January 1
of those years. However, if these figures are taken at
their face value, they show the spectacular increase in
membership the Party enjoyed during the first few years
after the Pérez Jiménez regime, and the equally spectacular decline during the four years' resort to violence.

No detailed data are available that break down Communist Party membership in terms of age, sex, race,
education, or other criteria. However, some general
observations on the subject can be made.

The age and class composition of the Communist
movement evidently changed considerably between its two

138

periods of legality, in the 1940's and from 1958 to 1962.
During the earlier period Communist membership undoubtedly had a strong working-class bias; the majority of the
Party may well have been drawn from the ranks of organized labor at that time, and the average age of members
undoubtedly was higher than during 1958-62.

After the fall of the Pérez Jiménez dictatorship, the
increase in Party membership was particularly notable
among university students, especially in the Federal District (Caracas). At the same time, the Party acquired a
new kind of member, previously rare, the shanty-town
dweller in the barrios of Caracas and in the environs of
other major cities. These people were seldom regularly
employed and unlikely to be trade union members.

Another significant difference between the pre- and
post-Pérez Jiménez periods was the decline in the once
substantial Communist influence, and presumably Party
membership, among the oil workers. Finally, no substantial change took place between the two periods in the
relatively small number of peasants in Communist ranks.

The leadership of the Communist Party has tended to
come from all ranks of society, although for the kind of
party the PCV pretends to be, it has had a disproportion-
ately high percentage of upper-class members. A look
at a few typical leaders may throw some light on the nature of PCV leadership.

From the earliest days of Venezuelan communism,
the Machado brothers, Gustavo and Eduardo, have been
among the top echelon. They come from a wealthy family,
and when they are not in hiding, in jail, or in exile, they
reside in one of the more fashionable sections of Caracas.
They are well educated, world-travelled, and somewhat
debonair in their behavior. Their political opponents not

infrequently make fun of their role as "proletarian" leaders, and similar criticisms are not unknown even in Communist Party ranks.

Among the younger leaders, an outstanding figure is Teodoro Petkoff. Of middle-class immigrant background, he rose to importance in Party councils as a leader of the Juventud Comunista in the Central University of Caracas. He was one of the younger men—along with trade unionist Eloy Torres—to be co-opted onto the Communist ticket for deputies in the 1958 election. For a while one of the most furious Leftists in the party, he has recently become a leader of the movement away from violence.

Of an entirely different type from either the Machados or Petkoff are such working-class Communist leaders as Jesús Faria and Cruz Villegas. The former was converted to communism soon after the death of dictator Juan Vicente Gómez. During the dictatorship he was an illiterate oil worker. The Party is said to have taught him to read and write. They recognized his leadership potential very early, and he was for years an outstanding figure among the trade unionists of the oil fields. Whatever influence the Communists still have in that area is largely due to Faria.

Cruz Villegas, a small mulatto from Caracas, is a former mosaic worker who first emerged as a leader of his own trade group. Although literate, he has little formal education. His influence in the Party, and such prestige as he still commands in organized labor, stems from his shrewdness, his ability as a union leader, organizer, and negotiator, and his oratorical powers.

Of still a different type is Rodolfo Quintero. He was a student who belonged to the "generation of '28, " the young men who seized the presidential palace in an unsuccessful attempt to overthrow the Gómez dictatorship in 1928. When he returned to political activity after Gómez' death, he was a Communist, and chose organized labor as his field of work. He gained a considerable influence among the workers of Caracas, who appreciated his organizational and oratorical abilities. He has been a leading Communist trade unionist ever since.

The leadership has been top-heavy with middle- and upper-class people. In 1961, of the eighty-man Central Committee only Rodolfo Quintero, Cruz Villegas, and Eloy Torres were well known Communist trade unionists. Jesús Faria, the Party's Secretary General, had been a leading labor figure, but for a decade had functioned as a Party bureaucrat. The rest of the members had little contact with organized labor in spite of their claims to be leaders of "the party of the proletariat."

EFFECTIVENESS OF COMMUNIST LEADERSHIP

The effectiveness of the Venezuelan Communist leadership has depended largely upon the demands it has made on its followers. So long as the Party operated principally in the trade unions, the peasant organizations, and the barrios of Caracas and other cities, the party membership loyally followed its leaders' directives. In fact, the lower echelons in most of these sectors stuck by the national chiefs even when the Party instigated the violence after 1961. The barrio leaders tried to arouse their supporters, even though they realized that in doing so they would probably destroy their own influence among their neighbors.

But for the most part, the results of the 1962-66 period indicate that the Party rank and file were reluctant to follow their leaders into violent conflict with the elected regime. Virtually all the guerrillas and urban terrorists seem to have been university and high school students, almost none were workers, and the guerrillas were notoriously unsuccessful in recruiting peasants.

Not only were the worker and peasant members of the Communist Party reluctant to take the violent road to power, they were, as we have seen, even dilatory in paying their dues. Dues-paying is the minimum expression of loyalty to an organization like the Communist Party, which demands an extraordinarily high degree of discipline, loyalty, and participation from its members. The lag in dues payments reported in 1963 and 1964, therefore, was an eloquent expression of the inability of the PCV leaders to persuade their members to follow a policy that was unpopular among the rank and file.

Chapter Four

THE VENEZUELAN EXPERIMENT

A priori, Venezuela would appear to be a propitious country for the rise of a successful Communist Party. A nation of marked contrasts and extremes of wealth and poverty, undergoing rapid social and economic change, and with a weak tradition of stable democratic government, Venezuela during recent decades has certainly experienced widespread popular discontent. Furthermore, its location relative to the Panama Canal and its vast petroleum resources give it a strategic importance which should have heightened the interest of the international Communist movement in the success of its Venezuelan affiliate. However, the history of the PCV shows it has been unable to capitalize on the advantages it seemed to possess.

PHYSICAL AND HUMAN GEOGRAPHY

Venezuela is one of the large South American countries in area, encompassing 352,143 square miles. The Orinoco River, the second largest in South America, meanders through the southern half of the country and finds its outlet to the sea in a wide delta near the eastern border of Venezuela with Guyana. Over most of this region, the climate is humid and tropical, and the land is covered with almost impenetrable jungle, which until the early 1950's constituted a serious barrier to settlement. However, in recent decades great mineral resources have invited the development of mining and industry in an area long inhabited mainly by primitive Indians.

The Andes form the Colombian frontier in the west, then alter their roughly north-south alignment eastward along the coast, dribbling out in islands such as Margarita and Trinidad off the Caribbean shore. The mountains are interspersed with valleys, particularly in the west, and these are some of the most heavily populated parts of the country.

In the central part of the country, just south of the main line of mountains west of Caracas, is a wide valley, with Lake Valencia in its center. This is one of the most intensively cultivated agricultural regions in the nation, and a major population center as well. In recent years the cities of this region have developed rapidly and have become centers of diversified industry. Caracas, the national capital and by far the largest concentration of population, lies along three valleys forming a "Y" just behind the coastal mountain range. Except in the western frontier area, most Venezuelans have traditionally lived within a few score miles of the sea, in valleys of or behind the Andes.

In the northwestern segment of the country lies Lake Maracaibo. Most of the nation's oil reserves are in and around the lake, and on its shores are the city of Maracaibo and other towns dependent on the oil industry. Beyond the cities and towns is a flat region which is increasingly devoted to grazing.

Finally, among the major geographical features of Venezuela are the "llanos," the great plains which spread south and east of the Andes and merge into the jungle of the Orinoco Valley region. This is an area famous in legend and story for the exploits of the "llaneros," the counterparts of the North American cowboys and the gauchos of Argentina. It is another area, like the Orinoco Valley, which has just begun to develop economically.

The estimated population of Venezuela in 1966 was 9,189,200. A cabinet member once summed up the racial situation in the country to the author by saying, "We are all café au lait, some more café and others more au lait. " The great majority of the population has both African and European ancestry.

Most of the European background is Spanish. However, there is also a strong admixture of people from outlying Spanish possessions, particularly the Canary Islands. During the present century hundreds of thousands of Italian and Portuguese immigrants have also settled in Venezuela, and the older ones especially have integrated well into Venezuelan society.

The Negro ancestors of present-day Venezuelans were brought from Africa originally to work sugar, coffee and other plantations during the colonial period. East of Caracas are areas where the Negro population live largely as their forefathers did on the Dark Continent. Racial mixture between Negroes and whites began very early, and even many of the "best" families have at least some African ancestry. The Spanish historian and biographer Salvador de Madariaga claims that Simón Bolivar himself was a mulatto. [1]

The Indian population is small. Most pure-blooded Indians live in the area west of Lake Maracaibo and in the jungles of the Orinoco Valley. However, sizable numbers of people of mixed Indian-white background live in the mountainous western states of Táchira, Mérida, and Trujillo, and in the llanos.

THE VENEZUELAN ECONOMY

Until World War I Venezuela had a predominantly agricultural economy, in which most of the population were subsistence farmers, producing only enough for their families' needs, and having little to sell. Some large commercial farms produced cacao, coffee, and tobacco, which constituted the largest part of the nation's exports.

The urban population was a small minority. The only major city was the capital, Caracas, although in the interior were various other towns of more or less importance, such as Barcelona and Maracaibo. Transportation facilities were primitive and sparse; there were no railways.

However, at the end of World War I vast resources of petroleum were discovered in and around Lake Maracaibo. Shortly afterward, oil was also discovered in the eastern state of Anzoátegui, although not on the scale of the Lake Maracaibo deposits.

The discovery of petroleum completely transformed the economy of Venezuela. By the late 1930's the production and export of oil was by far the most important economic activity in the country, accounting for almost all the nation's exports, providing directly and indirectly most of the government revenues, offering the largest source of nonagricultural employment, and generating a great deal of new economic activity not directly connected with the oil fields.

The sudden rise of the oil industry—within little more than a decade—brought many new problems. For one thing, foreign oil companies exploited Venezuela's petroleum resources. They provided not only capital, but

146

also management and most of the technicians. This large intrusion of foreigners into the economy generated considerable nationalistic resentment. Although the contribution made by American and British firms to oil development was widely recognized, it was generally felt that the companies were getting too much and Venezuela too little from its resources; that these alien interests had too much power in the nation's politics; that they took too little interest in the effects of their operations on the general economy and society of Venezuela.

The oil industry created a number of additional difficulties. The tendency of relatively high wages in the oil fields to attract workers from other segments of the economy, particularly from agriculture, resulted in a distortion of the pre-petroleum economy. Still more important, successive governments tended to concentrate their attention and their expenditures on the oil areas and the national capital, virtually ignoring other sectors, notably agriculture. Finally, it was almost universally agreed that dependence on a single export industry created perils for the country, and that economic diversification was necessary and desirable.

But if oil development and the leading role it gave to foreign firms tended to stimulate the rapid growth of nationalism, it also brought into existence a sizable wage-earning working class, not only in the oil fields but also in certain cities and towns where it quickened the pace of the economy. In addition, it fostered the growth of the middle class, of merchants, professional people, and even pioneer industrialists.

Finally, oil provided the Venezuelan government with financial resources undreamed of by governments before 1918. These relatively ample funds gave the government a dominant role in the national economy. Since an increasingly large proportion of the total national income accrued to the government through taxes, royalties, and other imposts on oil, the way these funds were spent could profoundly influence all segments of economic activity.

Taken together, these developments provided most of the issues which dominated Venezuelan politics in the decades following the death of dictator Juan Vicente Gómez in 1935. Economic nationalism, growing demands by unions and other groups for social reforms, the distribution of government revenue were matters of continuous bitter dispute among political parties and other groups active in national politics.

In recent years the Venezuelan economy has become a good deal more diversified. The proportionate share of petroleum in the gross national product has slightly declined, while manufacturing has increased. The role of public utilities has also expanded somewhat. Agriculture declined during the 1950's, but has recovered somewhat in importance since then. The figures in Table 3 are from the Economic Survey of Latin America 1964 (p. 116), published by the United Nations Economic Commission for Latin America. The data were provided by CORDIPLAN, the Venezuelan government planning agency.

SOCIAL CONDITIONS

Despite a long tradition of political tyranny in Venezuela, a considerable degree of social democracy exists, largely because of the civil wars of the nineteenth century. The Wars of Independence themselves were terribly costly in lives, especially of upper-class Venezuelans, who led the struggle against the Spaniards. Subsequently, in the 1860's the Federal War was fought, ostensibly over the issue of whether Venezuela should be a federal or unitary republic, but in fact it was a social war in which a large part of the

Table 3

Venezuelan Gross National Product

Sector	% of 1950	Gross 1958	Domestic Product 1960	Product 1964
Agriculture	8.5	7.0	7.3	7.4
Mining	0.2	1.8	2.1	1.3
Petroleum	25.9	24.8	24.8	23.8
Manufacturing	9.6	11.5	11.6	13.4
Construction	4.6	4.8	3.9	3.9
Electricity, gas and water	0.6	1.2	1.4	1.9
Government	6.6	4.0	3.6	4.1
Other services	44.0	44.8	45.4	44.8
Transport and communications	5.7	4.3	4.1	3.8
Trade	11.8	13.8	12.6	12.5
Housing	10.2	11.2	12.1	11.5
Miscellaneous	16.3	15.5	16.6	16.4

traditional landed elite were physically destroyed and those remaining lost much of their wealth and property.

As a result of these conflicts, there is today in Venezuela virtually no traditional landowning aristocracy which has held the land since the early years of the Spanish Conquest, as there is in neighboring Colombia and in most other Latin American countries. Although there are rich Venezuelans, indeed very rich ones, their wealth has been acquired during the last two or three generations. These people live exceedingly well, materially speaking, but they do not have the disdain toward poorer members of society evinced by the traditional aristocrats of neighboring countries. Nor do they believe that the only appropriate employment for a gentleman is directing work on the land. Their investments in industry, public utilities, and trade far exceed those in land.

There is a much wider degree of social intercourse among different classes in Venezuela than in many other Latin American countries. The economically lower classes of the country lack the subservience characteristic of those Latin American countries with a still powerful landed oligarchy.

But the relative social democracy in Venezuela has its limits. Race consciousness still exists, although it seems to be declining. Thus, in 1945 when Rómulo Betancourt, the leader of the new Acción Democrática government, appointed a pronouncedly mulatto colleague to his cabinet, this action was criticized. However, there was little criticism of Betancourt's own racial background (although he was known to be a mulatto) because his Negro ancestry was not visually apparent. Since 1945, several other distinct mulattoes have been top figures in the government.

The majority of Venezuelans now live in towns and cities. Between 1950 and 1960 the urban population increased from 2.4 million people, or 49% of the total, to 4.5 million or 62%. In the ten-year period, the rural segment increased in numbers from 2.4 million people to 2.8 million, but declined in percentage from 51% to 38%. [2]

The Venezuelan population contains several well-defined groupings. At the top of the social scale are the families which dominate the nationally owned segments of the economy. These include the Mendoza, Volmer, Bolton consortia. Each of these has interests in various branches of the economy, including manufacturing, banking, real

150

estate, importing, local commerce, and some in agriculture. Members of these families also play a leading role in the professions.

This leading social and economic group has many purely domestic enterprises, but in others it is in partnership with foreign companies. Some members of the group are now minority members on the boards of directors of Venezuelan affiliates of foreign oil companies.

The Venezuelan middle class includes much of the professional group, small businessmen, most government employees, the many privately employed white collar workers, and most military officers.

A third urban element is the wage-earning working class, employed in the nation's growing industries, in transport and communications, in the mining camps and petroleum fields, and in construction. Both manual workers and large elements among white collar workers have been organized since 1958 into the large and powerful trade union movement.

Finally, there is the growing population of the slums or "barrios" which ring Caracas and most other urban centers. These people live in houses they have built themselves, ranging from lean-tos constructed in one night of packing boxes and similar materials, to sturdier structures of concrete blocks. Although some barrio dwellers are fully employed, a large proportion are casual laborers, particularly those employed part time in the construction industry, or self-employed salesmen of everything from combs to lottery tickets.

The rural areas also embrace several well defined groups. Most of the remaining large landowners do not live regularly on their estates. However, approximately a quarter of a million small or medium sized landlords cultivate their own acres. These include 130,000 or more farm families who were settled on their own land by the Instituto Agrario Nacional after 1958. There are still tens of thousands of poor peasants, known as "conqueros," who live as squatters on land belonging to large proprietors or to the government. This group will presumably be converted into small property holders within a few years as agrarian reform continues. Finally, a group of some importance consists of agricultural wage earners who cultivate large sugar estates and other major commercial farming enterprises, some of which belong to the government.

A special place in the class structure is held by foreigners working for foreign companies operating in Venezuela. These include high officials and technicians of the oil and iron-mining companies, managerial personnel of foreign-owned manufacturing enterprises, and ranking officials and some subordinate personnel in other firms, such as accounting, banking, and the like. They are an important element in the national economy and mix socially with upper-class, sometimes with middle-class, Venezuelans. However, they are on the Venezuelan scene in an essentially temporary capacity, and they must exercise considerable caution to avoid endangering their employers' positions in the country.

COMMUNISTS' ANALYSIS OF VENEZUELAN SOCIAL STRATIFICATION

The Communist analysis of the various classes which make up Venezuelan society is somewhat more simplistic than the one we have presented. They divide the society into four basic groups: the working class, the capitalist class, the peasants, and the middle class. [3]

The working class is defined by Guillermo García Ponce, PCV Politburo member, in orthodox Marxist terms as "composed of men and women without any property in the means of production and obliged, in consequence, to sell for wages their labor force to the capitalists." The Communist Party, it is asserted, "is a unit for combat of the working class. Its organized unit— conscious, in the vanguard. It is the highest form of organization of the working class. Its General Staff."

The capitalist class (or bourgeoisie) "is composed of the proprietors and owners of the means of production (factories, machines, mines, etc.), who contract the labor force of the workers to put in action their means of production; that is to say, they exploit wage labor." Within the capitalist class are the large landholders (latifundistas) who are composed of "proprietors of great quantities of land and live from the income produced by the peasants who work these. . . . This income can be in specie, money or labor."

The peasantry, say the Communists, are "those who live from labor in agriculture," but the peasantry "does not form a homogeneous mass." They should be subdivided into "semiproletarians," those who work "part of the year as wage earners . . . and the rest as individual conuqueros"; the "poor peasants, who work all the time as conuqueros, squatters. . . ." It is added that "there exist also middle and rich peasants, who are differentiated from the rest because they produce for the market and employ wage labor. Some are proprietors of land, but the majority rent it from the large landholders."

The middle classes, or petty bourgeoisie, consist of "men and women who occupy an intermediary position between the working class and the capitalists. Some have certain means of production as artisans, and others live

153

independently from their skilled work. They consist of "the artisans, the small merchants, and a certain part of the professionals." However, it is added that "the exploited groups of white collar workers, journalists, and professionals who sell their labor force to capitalist enterprises or to the State belong to the working class."

Special attention is paid to "the dominant and exploiting classes in Venezuela." These are defined as "the great imperialist bourgeoisie, the capitalists, and the latifundistas." Within these, special attention is given to "the great foreign imperialist bourgeoisie." Of them, it is said "they not only exploit the Venezuelan working class (in petroleum, iron, etc.) but they exploit the whole Venezuelan Nation, deform its economy and its commerce, politically oppress the country. They not only exploit the Venezuelan workers, but the workers of all the capitalist countries. They are the Rockefellers, Morgans, Duponts, Reynolds, etc., the great owners of the Standard (Creole) Oil Company, the National City Bank, General Motors, etc."

This Communist analysis of Venezuelan class structure is notable for two things. First, it borrows heavily from the Russian model, particularly in dividing peasants among poor, middle, and rich categories. Second, it is oblivious to the substantial changes which have come about in the Venezuelan economy in recent decades, particularly the emergence of manufacturing.

The picture of Venezuelan government and political life which the PCV draws is orthodox Marxist-Leninist. García Ponce defined the State as "a group of institutions and instruments in the hands of dominant and exploiting classes for the purpose of defending the existing regime and its own class interests, and maintaining the domination and exploitation of the rest of society." More specifically, the Venezuelan state is defined as being "at the service of the imperialists, large capitalists, and latifundistas. These are the economically most powerful classes and those which dominate the national and international policy of Venezuela. The social exploiting and dominant classes use the State to maintain the workers, peasants, middle classes, and other popular sectors of the population in a condition of domination and exploitation."

The role of the Communist Party is to change this situation, to "substitute for the present State, which is at the service of the imperialists, large capitalists and latifundistas, a New State, the National, Patriotic, Democratic, and Popular State which consequently will be at the service of the popular classes, of the workers, peasants, middle classes and other progressive sectors within Venezuelan society. In it the interests of these social classes will be decisive. In it all the institutions and instruments of the State will be at the service of the people."

Needless to say, this definition does not recognize the great influence of the organized labor and peasant sectors in Acción Democrática, the party in power when García Ponce was writing. Nor does it recognize that the AD government was bringing about substantial changes in the existing economy and society, particularly through its programs of agrarian reform and social development in the rural areas.

MINORITY GROUPS

The Venezuelan population contains only two important minority groups: the recent immigrants and the dwellers in the barrios. The first is a relatively marginal group certain to decline in importance, the second constitutes one of the country's major economic, social, cultural, and political problems.

After World War II immigrants streamed into Venezuela. Some were displaced persons who sought refuge, but most came from southern Europe either because they were attracted by the oil prosperity of the 1950's or because they hoped to use Venezuela as a stepping stone to the United States.

Immigration was particularly heavy during the Pérez Jiménez dictatorship. Workers frequently came to labor on the government's public works programs, sometimes to work for their Italian employers who had contracts from the Venezuelan regime. They stayed to become petty merchants, taxicab drivers, or workers of other kinds.

The extent of immigration during the 1950's is demonstrated by statistics concerning the number of foreign-born residents in 1950 and in 1961. The United Nations Demographic Yearbook 1956 gives a total of 208,731 for 1950; the Demographic Yearbook 1963 gives 556,875 for 1961. This represents an increase in foreign-born residents in Venezuela of 348,144, or more than 250 percent, during the decade of the 1950's.

This immigrant group was resented by many lower-class Venezuelans. They complained that many immigrants were taking the best paid and most skilled manual positions away from natives. The immigrants were further disliked because, under threat of deportation—or worse—they were forced to collaborate closely with the dictatorship. Their unanimity in voting for Pérez Jiménez in the 1957 "plebiscite," for instance, was widely resented.

During the 1960's the immigration stream has slackened. It seems unlikely, considering the rapid natural increase in the Venezuelan population, the continuing problem of unemployment, and the persistent, albeit reduced, migration of rural folk to the large cities, that there will be any great influx of immigrants in the foreseeable future. Thus it seems likely that the immigrants who remain in Venezuela will be readily absorbed into the population.

The Venezuelan Communists have not succeeded in penetrating the immigrant group, nor is there much indication that they have tried to do so. The immigrants have generally avoided becoming involved in Venezuelan politics, and the few who have, have tended to join one of the larger parties.

The other "minority" group, the barrio dwellers, present a more serious problem, and will likely remain one much longer. The barrio people are native Venezuelans, of various racial backgrounds, and were not recognized as a "minority" while they lived in the interior of the country, but the difficulty of their current economic and social position certainly constitutes a major minority problem.

The occupants of the shanty-towns which one can see on all the hills about Caracas, and which exist somewhat less spectacularly in most other cities, are a marginal element in Venezuelan society, and a potentially explosive one. Their housing is precarious; as yet only a few are served by rudimentary public utilities; most of them are not regularly employed.

The barrio dwellers arrived in such large numbers after the Pérez Jiménez dictatorship that it was impossible to provide them with employment or their barrios with running water and other services. Governments have been well aware of the problem, but have been able to make only a bare beginning at coping with it.

The Betancourt government for a while at least, chose

quite deliberately not to make a major effort to improve conditions in the barrios. The reasoning behind this policy was that a major attack on conditions in the barrios would prove fruitless unless something was first done to slow down the migration to the cities. Indeed, it might be counterproductive without such an effort in the interior of the country. If conditions were not improved in agriculture, and in the small towns and hamlets of the interior, a major attack on the barrio problem would only serve to induce still larger numbers of migrants to Caracas and other major cities, and would intensify rather than mitigate the problem.

Hence, the Betancourt regime concentrated on trying to improve conditions in the hinterland. Vast programs for bringing electricity, schools, water supplies, sewerage, housing, and medical facilities combined with the agrarian reform program to make life in the interior more attractive, and hence, hopefully, to slow down the drift to Caracas and other cities. Only in the last year of his regime did Betancourt begin to pay major attention to the barrio problem. His successor, President Leoni, has done rather more for the barrios, but the barrio dwellers remain a potential time bomb in the center of Venezuelan society.

Although, as we have noted, the Partido Comunista and the MIR failed in the early 1960's to convert the barrios into hotbeds of revolutionary activity, this failure stemmed from conditions then current which well may no longer hold. Two factors were of primary importance: first, despite their miserable living conditions, the barrio dwellers were for the most part better off than they had been, and the barrio represented a movement upward on the social and economic scale; second, although the barrio residents were disillusioned in Acción Democrática and had never believed in its coalition partner, Copei, they still had faith in the democratic system propounded by several of the opposition parties, especially by Admiral Larrazábal's Frente Democrático Popular and by Arturo Uslar Pietri's independent grouping which after the election of 1963 became the Frente Nacional Democrático.

Whether or not the barrio dwellers will become a major revolutionary danger to the present regime, and hence perhaps a prime recruiting ground for the Partido Comunista de Venezuela and for groups to its left, will largely depend upon whether barrio conditions can be improved with sufficient rapidity to maintain the hopes of the inhabitants. This, in turn, will depend on the progress of the Venezuelan economy.

Talton Ray, in his excellent survey, already cited, of political life in the barrios, suggests that maintaining the barrio dwellers' faith in the democratic system will become complicated with the second generation of these people. Not having had the experience of moving from worse conditions in the rural areas, the younger generation will have only their own aspirations for improvement against which to measure their current living and working conditions. If these aspirations cannot be met, at least to a reasonable degree, the barrio "minority" in the population may well become a menace to the whole effort of recent years to establish a solidly based democratic society and government.

VENEZUELAN BELIEF SYSTEM

The vast majority of Venezuelans are nominally followers of Roman Catholicism. However, this fact in and of itself does not seem to this writer to be a major barrier to the penetration of the Communist Party and its growth in the country. Recent developments within the Roman Catholic Church have tended to blur somewhat the former apparently irreconcilable conflict between Catholicism and Marxism-Leninism.

Furthermore, the hold of the Catholic Church on the people of Venezuela, except perhaps in the three mountain states of Trujillo, Mérida, and Táchira, is too slight to constitute much of a barrier to the penetration of an ideology and a political organization which would seem to provide an answer to Venezuela's pressing social and economic problems.

The Church in Venezuela suffers from the same handicaps as it does in most of Latin America. Its "faithful" are at best nominal members of the Church, baptized, married, and perhaps buried in the Church, but having relatively little contact with it the rest of the time. The Church is badly understaffed in all of Latin America.

The Church is not wealthy, and although it is still the "established" church in Venezuela, it receives little support from the government. For instance, in 1965 federal government grants to "non-profit organizations" totaled only 36 million bolivares, or less than $10 million, and it cannot be presumed that the Church received all of this.[4]

During the nineteenth century the struggle over the secular power of the Church was a principal dividing line of national politics. However, in recent decades this issue has been relatively unimportant, except in the three mountain states. Thus, although Acción Democrática is a formally anticlerical party, and the Partido Social Cristiano Copei has a program based philosophically on the social teachings of the Catholic Church, the two parties worked in coalition, faced as they were by opponents on both Right and Left, throughout the Betancourt administration from 1959 to 1964.

The greatest strength of the Church in Venezuela is perhaps the fact that its leaders there awoke earlier than in most Latin American countries to the necessity for concerning themselves with the material needs and aspirations of the average layman. Thus both clergymen and laymen closely associated with the Church leadership have become deeply involved in labor unions, peasant organizations, cooperatives, credit unions, and Christian Democratic politics. In this last field, the Copei has a certain special appeal for those who still consider themselves good Catholics, as the party presents a political philosophy which seems to go beyond everyday economic and social problems, and to be based on a creed which also fulfills man's spiritual needs.

Generally speaking, Venezuelan Catholics are anti-Communist. However, only in the traditional communities of the states of Táchira, Mérida, and Trujillo, is communism seen as the embodiment of the antichrist, and anti-Communism as a sort of religious crusade. Elsewhere, the Catholic argument against communism tends to be in terms of opposition to totalitarianism, which, it is argued, stands in fundamental contrast to the Christian belief in each man's right to freedom and the pursuit of his own destiny.

The prevalence of nominal Catholicism has not prevented the widespread dissemination of elements of Marxism-Leninism. A belief in the class nature of society, in the ultimate validity of Lenin's analysis of imperialism, is almost universal among intellectuals and literate working-class groups. These ideas, shared by Catholics and non-Catholics alike, are of course highly realistic in the Venezuelan context, where great class differences are obvious, and where the economy for two generations has been overwhelmingly dominated by an oil industry almost completely in foreign hands.

However, the widespread belief in certain elements of Marxism-Leninism does not mean that most intellectuals or most urban workers have been automatically attracted to the Communist Party. Quite the contrary. Because the Communist Party is closely associated in the minds of its own members and of the public at large with the Soviet Union, there is a widespread tendency to look upon it as merely the agency of another imperialism, opposed to the one which dominates the nation's economy, but not necessarily preferable because of that.

The Communist interpretation of Marxism-Leninism thus conflicts with an even more widespread ideology: nationalism. If there is a single ideology which is virtually universal in Venezuelan society, it is nationalism. A fundamental belief is that the country must follow its own path, seeking its own answers to its own peculiar problems, and not follow the lead of any group which, like the Communists, appears to owe allegiance to some other nation. This is a principle of both Acción Democrática and Copei, and is shared by most other groups participating in national politics.

Politically alert Venezuelans thus have concentrated their attention on the problems of their own country. This tendency was reinforced by the bitter struggle against the dictatorship in the 1950's, and by ensuing efforts to establish a stable democratic regime. During these two trying periods, Venezuelans were relatively uninterested in world problems around which the Communists tried to build campaigns, such as the "peace" issue which for so many years has been the subject of Communist attention.

THE VENEZUELAN POLITICAL SYSTEM

In form, Venezuela is a constitutional democratic republic. In practice, it has been something else during

162

most of the time since the nation gained independence. It is a startling fact that Rómulo Betancourt, who served as constitutional president from 1959 to 1964, was the first president in Venezuelan history both to come into office through democratic elections and to turn over his office to a democratically elected successor.

No other country in Latin America has a worse history of military rule and political tyranny than Venezuela. Throughout most of the nineteenth century the characteristic leader was the "caudillo," a familiar type, in most Central American and some South American countries during the same period. He was a charismatic individual with considerable local economic power, which enabled him to command support from a sizable group of men who would take up arms at his call. He was also one who had the ability to inspire loyalty even beyond the sphere of his local influence. The typical caudillo organized more or less absolute power in one segment of a Venezuelan state; if he possessed sufficient ambition, audacity, popular following, and luck, he might seize control of a whole state. An extraordinary caudillo would lead his motley following in a descent upon the capital which, if successful, would result in his becoming President of the Republic until he was overthrown by another caudillo.

The last of these caudillo presidents was Juan Vicente Gómez, who seized power in 1909 and remained in control until he died peacefully in bed in December 1935. During his administration two things occurred which changed Venezuela and ended the caudillo system. One was the discovery and exploitation of the vast petroleum reserves, which catapulted Venezuela into an oil boom that inevitably undermined the foundations of the old rurally based caudillo system of politics.

The second notable event of the Gómez period was his

establishment of a military academy, which began to turn out career officers some time before Gómez left the scene. Although the transformation of the military from a group of of free booters following a highly personalist leader into a professional officer corps did not end the series of military tyrants, it did transform military rule—particularly during the 1948-58 period—from control by an all-powerful caudillo whose authority rested in his personal following and his cleverness, to a much more institutionalized system, in which the dictator became the first among equals within the top leadership of the officer group. Pérez Jiménez, in contrast to Cipriano Castro, Juan Vicente Gómez, or other caudillo predecessors, lacked charisma, and was ultimately overthrown not by a rival caudillo but by the leaders of the officer corps, who felt he had outlived his usefulness and was endangering the whole military institution.

Since the death of Gómez, new forces in the form of political parties, trade unions, professional associations, peasant organizations, organized student groups, and many more, have appeared on the political scene. These have broadened the base of political power. Although the military leadership is still capable of seizing power, it must gain the acquiescence of many civilian groups to maintain control for any length of time. Loyalty to a regime, or at least acquiescence in it, now depends more on material self-interest than on attachment to the person of the leader, as it did before 1935.

In spite of the setback of the 1948-58 period, Venezuela has been evolving toward a stable democracy. The first stage of this evolution was the 1941-48 period, when under Medina Angarita the bonds of the preceding dictatorship were greatly relaxed and all political groups had freedom to operate. Under the Acción Democrática regime the great masses of the people were given an active role in political life that they had never enjoyed before.

The second phase in the development of Venezuelan democracy has come since 1958. After a year-long Provisional Government following the overthrow of Pérez Jiménez in January 1958, the election, one of the freest in the country's history, brought to power a regime which under two successive presidents has continued to rule.

Presidents Rómulo Betancourt and Raúl Leoni have both been pledged to a broad-gauged program of social reform and economic development, whose basic outlines we have described in an earlier part of this work. It has involved agrarian reform, vastly expanded educational and health facilities, and extension of the basic needs of modern society to large segments of the population that had never before enjoyed them.

It has also involved a major effort to diversify the economy so as to reduce its dependence upon petroleum, through developing both the agricultural and manufacturing sectors. Through this program, the contribution of petroleum to the gross national product has been reduced from 23.1% in 1957 to 20.6% in 1965, while manufacturing has risen from 13.4% to 17.6%.[5] Even more significant, the country has been made virtually self-sufficient in a wide range of products, from foodstuffs to pharmaceuticals and metallurgical products, which it imported only a few years ago. It has even begun to export modest amounts of manufactured goods.

Finally, the Betancourt-Leoni regime has followed a nationalist policy, particularly with regard to petroleum. It has established a national oil company and has been preparing the way for national interests eventually to take over the foreign-owned oil properties and installations.

All these measures have helped to strengthen the foundation for a stable democratic regime. It is perhaps significant that Betancourt had to face four major military insurrections during his term of office, in addition to innumerable plots that were frustrated short of open rebellion, whereas the Leoni administration has faced not a single major and only one minor uprising. Although predictions are risky in a country like Venezuela, with its long tradition of military rule, it seems possible that if the reform and development program in existence since 1959 can continue for another full term after Leoni, a new tradition of stable, democratic government, in which legally elected administrations succeed one another, may well be established.

The success so far of the Betancourt-Leoni experiment has certainly increased the popularity of the democratic system, and has contributed to the growing conviction among broad segments of the population that stable democracy is feasible for Venezuela. Its success, too, has proved a major stumbling block to the progress of political extremists, in particular of the Communist Party. As we noted in the historical section of this monograph, the Partido Comunista de Venezuela contributed to the erosion of its own influence by its unsuccessful resort to major violence against the democratically elected regime; however, in view of the government's ability to meet some of the most pressing social demands and to foster rapid economic development it is doubtful whether the PCV could have made major progress against it even without the violence.

As it happened, the resort to violence was disastrous not only because it was aimed against a government which was carrying out a widely popular political program, but also because it was so clearly influenced by forces abroad. The Cuban government made no secret of its support of the urban terrorism and rural guerrilla war in which the Communists participated for four years. There was also widespread suspicion—however wrong it may have been—that the Soviet Union too was supporting this attempt to overthrow the democratically elected regime.

Venezuela has been peculiarly subject to pressures and pulls from abroad ever since the petroleum industry became the major source of its income. It is widely believed, and to a considerable extent it is true, that because the major oil companies in Venezuela are American (the British-owned Shell is the only exception), and because the United States is the most important market, Venezuelan governments are more subject to pressure from the United States than the government of any sovereign nation should be. However, resentment against what is considered the excessive influence of the United States has not made Venezuelans eager to throw themselves into the arms of some other foreign power, least of all a small Latin American one. The resentment against Cuban interference in internal Venezuelan affairs—which spread in 1966 into the ranks of the Venezuelan Communist Party—has been all but universal.

This resentment was perhaps intensified by the fact that the Betancourt-Leoni regime followed a foreign policy which obviously was not dictated by the United States. In the area of international petroleum policy, it took the lead in organizing a group of oil-producing countries with the common aim of maintaining the price of petroleum. In the Dominican Republic crisis of 1965, the Leoni government opposed United States military intervention. In general Latin American policy, Venezuela evolved "the Betancourt Doctrine," whereby it refused to recognize Latin American regimes which came to power by military coup, and urged this as an inter-American policy—something which the United States in particular was quite unwilling to adopt. The Venezuelan government, too, in 1966 led in organizing an informal bloc composed of Venezuela, Colombia, Peru, and Chile, one of whose purposes was to present a united front to the United States on a number of issues.

167

Chapter Five

PARTY CONFLICT AND INTEGRATION
WITH THE VENZUELAN ENVIRONMENT

The Communists of Venezuela have frequently resorted to violent methods in their struggle for power. In most such instances they had slight alternative in the face of a dictatorship which gave them little freedom of legal action. However, in the period 1962-66, as we have indicated repeatedly, the Partido Comunista de Venezuela resorted to various types of violence as the result of its own deliberate choice. During the 1962-66 period the party went to the extreme of accepting the idea that guerrilla warfare and urban terrorism were its principal, and almost exclusive, strategic weapons.

In at least three periods, the PCV has used or sought to use open revolution as its basic strategy for getting all or a share of power. These periods were between 1948 and 1951, during 1957, and during 1962-66.

After the overthrow of the Acción Democrática regime in November 1948, the leaders and members of the "Red" Communist Party, the PCV, worked fairly closely with the Acción Democrática underground, although the PCV itself remained legal until early 1950. During this period, as the Central Committee itself was to declare in a later "self-criticism," the party tended to place heavy reliance upon a possible military coup to overthrow the Junta Militar then in power. Acción Democrática still had numerous followers and friends in the officer corps of the armed forces, and they and the Red Communists sought to create conditions in which these could be mobilized to oust the regime.

As the Pérez Jiménez regime went through a crisis during 1957 over how to reelect the dictator, the PCV again attempted to capitalize on the situation to promote a military uprising against the regime. It collected what small arms it could, preparing for any eventuality. At the same time it entered into close cooperation with the underground organizations of Acción Democrática, Copei, and Unión Republicana Democrática in an effort to create an atmosphere of civil discontent and protest which would—as it eventually did—provoke the military into ending the dictatorship.

Then in 1962-66 the Partido Comunista de Venezuela launched a violent all-out attack on the democratically elected administrations of Presidents Rómulo Betancourt and Raúl Leoni. This effort went through three phases: coup d'etat, urban terrorism, and guerrilla warfare. All three failed.

The first phase of the resort to military violence in the 1960's was akin to the conspiratorial activities the PCV had participated in a decade or more earlier. Insurrections and attempted coups d'etat by elements of the armed forces, largely from the Navy and Marine Corps, in conjunction with the Communists and members of the Movimiento de Izquierda Revolucionaria, took place in May and June 1962 at Carúpano and Puerto Cabello. They were suppressed after a day's fighting in Carúpano, after several days' savage struggle in Puerto Cabello.

The Communists and their allies then switched their emphasis to urban terrorism on a minor scale, and launched some rural guerrilla actions at the same time. During 1962-63, when the effort was concentrated mainly in the cities, the party apparently hoped to create a situation which, as in 1957, would provoke the military into moving against the constituted government. This failed abysmally. The vast majority of registered voters participated in the election of 1963. The victor was President Betancourt's own party, Acción Democrática. The PCV and its allies then shifted to rural guerrilla warfare.

The guerrilla strategy differed in one essential from that of the urban terrorism: it was perforce a long-term undertaking with little hope of immediate success. Whereas urban terrorism was designed to get the military in a relatively short time to overthrow the elected government and to set up an unpopular regime, whereupon the extreme left would presumably be in a position to become leaders of a wide struggle against the regime, the emphasis of the guerrilla campaign was on destroying the armed forces and seizing power directly, a process which the Communists and their allies admitted would take years.

At various times the Communists have participated in or initiated other less military resorts to violence. At least thrice they have sought to use a partial or general strike to weaken or overthrow the regime. The first occasion was soon after the death of Juan Vicente Gómez, when Communists joined with other elements opposed to the López Contreras regime to launch a political general strike in Caracas in June 1936. This walkout, which spread to other major cities, had the frank objectives of forcing the regime to modify its policies in the direction of establishing political freedom and democracy. However, the walkout failed, at least in part because those responsible did not use it to bring down the government completely.

A second example of a widespread strike action by

groups including the Communists was the oil workers' walkout of early 1950. Acción Democrática's underground organized this strike, strongly supported by the Red Communists and less enthusiastically by the Blacks. It was called ostensibly over economic issues, but was certainly designed as the first step in a general move to overthrow the Junta Militar then in power. This effort also failed, in both its economic and its political objectives.

Finally, the PCV and MIR sought to convert a walkout of bank clerks in November 1960 into a general strike and a movement of "popular insurrection" against the Betancourt government. Since organized labor was largely controlled by Acción Democrática, President Betancourt's party, and the full weight of most trade union leaders was thrown against the call for a revolutionary general strike, it failed after a few days. This particular uprising was accompanied by a good deal of violence, which provoked the government to suspend some constitutional guarantees.

Thus, the violent road to power has never been notably successful for the Venezuelan Communists. Excepting the campaign against Pérez Jiménez in 1957, they have never succeeded in organizing or participating in a general strike or conspiratorial movement which toppled a government. Even in 1957-58, the Communists were part of a movement so broad that after the overthrow of the dictatorship the other parties involved more or less isolated the Communists from a decisive role in the new government.

Resort to more extreme methods has been even less successful. As we have indicated elsewhere, the use of urban terrorism and guerrilla war in the 1960's led to such a disastrous reduction in the power, influence, and general effectiveness of the Communist Party that after four years' experimentation with this strategy they finally abandoned it, at least for a while, in 1966-67, and returned to more peaceable methods of pursuing the struggle for power, including even, if possible, participation in elections.

CAUSES ESPOUSED BY COMMUNISTS

Over the years, the Communists have attempted at various times to associate themselves with causes which were popular with particular groups of their fellow countrymen or with the public in general. As conditions change, the party has tended to emphasize these causes more or less as it has judged them vital or fruitful for political advancement. We may note three such issues of particular and lasting significance: democracy, nationalism, and agrarian reform.

In view of the prolonged periods of dictatorship Venezuela has suffered, and the precarious nature of the country's democracy when it has existed at all, democracy versus right-wing and military dictatorship has been a fundamental national issue during the more than three and a half decades of the Communist movement's existence. At various times the Communists have sought to picture themselves as fellow democrats in the struggle against existing dictatorships, or as staunch supporters of democracy once dictatorial regimes have been overthrown.

During the military tyranny of the 1950's, the Communists frequently laid stress on their alleged wish for a return to democratic rule. Thus, late in 1952 the PCV appealed to Acción Democrática to form a united front against the regime. Three of the five points suggested as the platform for such a coalition were: "1. Re-establishment of constitutional guarantees. 2. Freeing of political prisoners. 3. Free elections presided over by a provisional government. "[1]

172

After the overthrow of the Pérez Jiménez dictatorship, the Communists insisted on their democratic good
faith and appealed to the nearly universal desire of Venezuelans for a stable constitutional and democratic regime.
In his pamphlet Introducción a la Política Venezolana,
already cited, PCV Political Bureau member Guillermo
García Ponce wrote:[2]

> The imperialists and the traditional dominant
> classes need terrorist governments and dictator-
> ships to increase the exploitation of Venezuela,
> and of the workers and peasants. For that rea-
> son they supported Gómez and brought to power
> Pérez Jiménez. They always seek to eliminate
> democratic liberties and to establish, through
> coups d'etat, repressive and despotic govern-
> ments.

> The Venezuelan people struggle for the forma-
> tion of a national and patriotic, popular and
> democratic government. There is necessary
> a Party which carries to its ultimate conse-
> quences the task of complete democratization
> of Venezuela, of its institutions and legisla-
> tion, of its politics and economy.

> THIS IS THE DEMOCRATIC BASIS FOR THE
> BIRTH OF THE COMMUNIST PARTY OF VENE-
> ZUELA.

Virtually all Venezuelans are more or less nationalistic. The Communists, in spite of their long-term attachment to the Soviet Union and their latter-day extolling of
Fidel Castro's regime, have sought almost from the beginning to exploit this deep-seated nationalistic sentiment.

Especially since World War II the Communists'

nationalistic appeal frequently has coincided with their basic commitment to the Soviet Union. It has been quite natural—given the pre-eminence of the United States in the Western Hemisphere and the power of U.S. firms in the Venezuelan economy—that Venezuelan nationalism should be turned against the United States. The Communists, in working to intensify this tendency, have also served well the interests of the Soviet Union in the Cold War.

The frame of reference for Venezuelan Communist attempts to exploit the nationalist issue is clearly revealed in the pamphlet of García Ponce, cited above:[3]

> After 1947 the penetration of Venezuela by imperialist capital was intensified, particularly on the part of the North American petroleum companies. There began the plundering on a large scale of the riches of Venezuela, the rape and extortion of the national economy.
>
> The very existence of the Venezuelan Nation has been endangered. The heritage of the Liberators is threatened with deformation by foreign colonization.
>
> As in 1810, against Spanish domination, there is now raised a national anti-imperialist consciousness, for defense of Venezuelan nationality, for struggle for independence and sovereignty of the Country.
>
> THIS IS THE NATIONAL BASIS FOR THE BIRTH OF THE COMMUNIST PARTY OF VENEZUELA

Quite understandably, the Communists have made their strongest nationalistic appeal on the issue of petroleum. This sector of the economy, which accounts for nearly half of Venezuela's income and most of its foreign exchange, is largely in the hands of foreign companies, all but one American. The depth of foreign investment and influence has provided a prime target for Communist attack.

The Communists have frequently accused the foreign companies of careless waste of exhaustible resources. Thus, in 1947, the then deputy of the Communist Party in the National Congress, Gustavo Machado, attacked specifically the burning of natural gas by the companies. He called this "a problem which does not require 'reasonable solutions,' but energetic, firm and audacious solutions. The Venezuelan people cannot permit, must not permit them to continue to burn 15% of Venezuela's petroleum production, without any benefit to either the productive classes or the industrial future of the country. This all demonstrates the magnitude of the disdain of the petroleum companies for Venezuela and its fundamental wealth. . . ."[4]

One of the interesting aspects of the running attack by Venezuelan Communists on the foreign-owned oil companies is that they never advocated complete nationalization of these firms. For instance, in a pamphlet published in Caracas soon after the fall of the Pérez Jiménez regime, Eduardo Machado, member of the Political Bureau of the Communist Party, praises those countries where the petroleum industry has been nationalized, but does not go on to advocate—except perhaps by implication—that Venezuela follow the same policy. He says:[5]

The great consortia presume that the exploitation of petroleum is possible only with their participation. This was a reality until the Soviet Union and then with its aid Rumania, Poland, China, etc., demonstrated that it was possible

175

to break the yoke of Royal Dutch Shell and
Standard Oil Company and to establish a petroleum industry on a more scientific basis, in
which the humanized socialist competition of
labor has guaranteed its enormous successes,
taking the place of the inhuman and ruinous
"rationalization" employed by the imperialists. Under different conditions, Mexico has
been able to nationalize its petroleum and exploit it with considerable advantage in spite of
intrigues and boycott by the foreign monopolies
which tended to create obstacles to the development of this Mexican industry.

These glowing descriptions notwithstanding, Machado
says nothing further about nationalization for Venezuela.

A third cause which has been popular in Venezuela for
several decades is agrarian reform. The Communists
have attempted to capitalize on this issue, particularly to
gain adherents among the peasantry. Typical of the appeal
they have made is the following passage from Guillermo
García Ponce's Introducción a la Política Venezolana.[6]

Latifundia signifies infraproduction of agriculture and grazing and infraconsumption of
the peasant masses, contributing a heavy
burden to the economic development of the
Country.

The liquidation of this situation demands the
realization of a radical and rapid Agrarian
Reform, which establishes peasant ownership
of the land, which liquidates latifundia and the
semifeudal relations which still persist, fixes
a maximum limit to the possession of land,
gives the land free of cost to the peasants in the

form of a family parcel . . . indicating to the
peasants the advantages of cooperative labor as
the only means of augmenting production and
productivity of the land in the face of the voracity
of capitalism in the countryside.

During the 1958-62 period, the Communist Party con-
tinually denounced the agrarian reform being carried out
by the Betancourt regime as "nonexistent." On various
occasions, they organized and led peasant invasions of
land, outside the provisions of the agrarian reform procedure, in the hope of embarrassing the government and
of getting the credit if the Agrarian Reform Institute finally
allowed the squatters to keep the areas they had seized.

However, these activities were not sufficient to gain
the Communists a large following in the countryside. The
peasants tended to believe—in spite of what the Communists told them and as a result of their experiences and
observations—that the agrarian reform effort of the Betancourt-Leoni government was genuine, and that eventually
every peasant would receive land.

Because of the ineffectiveness of Communist propaganda among the peasants in the face of the land distribution program of the regime, the Communists were able to
recruit only a handful of rural folk for their guerrilla efforts after 1962. The peasants were not then about to kill
the goose that was laying a golden egg.

BEHAVIOR OF PCV MEMBERS IN
LEGISLATIVE BODIES

Because of the illegal position of the PCV during a
large part of its history, the Communists have had little
legislative experience. However, during two periods they
did have members in Congress and in some of the sub-

ordinate legislative bodies. In the years 1946-47, two members of the Constituent Assembly were Communists, Gustavo Machado and Juan Bautista Fuenmayor, and they also served in the regular congress elected in 1947. Jesús Faria was elected senator in 1947. During this period, the Communist legislators were highly critical of the Acción Democrática regime, accusing it of violating national interests in dealing with foreign oil companies, and of mistreating the organized labor movement. However, they frequently defended the government against attacks from the right-wing opposition of the time, the Copei party.

In the election of December 1958, the PCV won one senatorship, again for Jesús Faria, and six seats in the Chamber of Deputies. They also elected members to a few state legislatures and city councils. In Caracas, they were the second largest bloc in the municipal council.

The Communist legislators held their seats even after the beginning of the extreme leftist violence, protected as they were by parliamentary immunity. Only Eloy Torres and Teodoro Petkoff, members of the Chamber of Deputies, were removed by that body itself and in accordance with constitutional procedure, after they were caught in flagrante delicto in insurrectional activities.

During the first two years of Betancourt's constitutional regime, when it was attacked principally from the extreme Right, Communist parliamentarians defended the democratic regime as such, although they were strongly critical of the coalition government. However, as the violence of the extreme Left against the Betancourt administration mounted in 1962 and 1963, the Communist legislators defended the coup attempts at Carúpano and Puerto Cabello, supported the subsequent urban terrorism of the PCV and MIR, and became uncompromisingly critical of the government. Few attacks on the regime by Communist deputies were based on reasoned and documented criticism of government policies. The PCV members of Congress were finally arrested in September 1963, three months before the general election. The proximate cause was a particularly outrageous incident of terrorism, the attack on a train just outside Caracas in which four National Guard members were murdered in cold blood.

ORGANIZATIONAL PERIPHERIES OF THE COMMUNIST MOVEMENT

The Communists have been active in an organized fashion in many different occupational and specific-issue groups ever since the end of the Juan Vicente Gómez dictatorship in the middle 1930's. In recent years, however, this kind of activity was severely curtailed with their concentration on the violent road to power. Too little time has elapsed since their withdrawal from the guerrilla struggle to know what degree of influence they will be able to regain in the various organizations where they lost it during the 1962-66 period.

The Communists of Venezuela have always pictured themselves as "the party of the workers. " It is therefore logical that during most of the party's existence they have given primary importance to penetrating the ranks of organized labor. Typical of the Venezuelan Communists' portrayal of themselves as the only real party of labor is the following passage from page 26 of Guillermo García Ponce's pamphlet Introducción a la Politica Venezolana:

With the appearance of capitalism (beginning of petroleum exploitation and establishment of some industries) the working class arose in Venezuela. The workers sold their labor force to the foreign and national capitalists, who used the workers to produce merchandise. The difference between

what the capitalists paid the workers as wages
and the value of the production created by the
labor of the workers (surplus value) is taken by
the capitalists and constitutes the source of their
wealth, the basis of the exploitation of the working class under capitalism.

It is necessary that there be a Party which struggles to free the working class from capitalist
exploitation, to defend the economic and historic
interests of the workers. The birth of the working class has demanded the formation of a new
party, the party of the working class.

THIS IS THE CLASS, SOCIAL, BASIS FOR THE
BIRTH OF THE COMMUNIST PARTY OF VENE-
ZUELA.

Communist influence in the organized labor movement
has varied a great deal from one epoch to another. During the first eight years or so following the death of Juan
Vicente Gómez, when the trade unions first appeared, Communist influence was dominant. Several of the most important Communist leaders—Jesús Faria, Rodolfo Quintero,
Luis Miquilena, Cruz Villegas—were closely associated
with the labor movement.

However, early in 1944 the Communists lost control
of the majority of organized labor to Acción Democrática.
In the years that followed, Communist influence was weakened even further by the split in Communist ranks: the
unions controlled by the so-called "Red" Communist Party
became more or less closely associated with those dominated by Acción Democrática, and participated in the formation of the Confederación de Trabajadores de Venezuela
in 1947; those under the influence of the "Black" Communist Partido Revolucionario Proletario (Comunista) were

organized in separate state federations in the Federal District and the state of Anzoátegui, where the Black Communist strength was principally concentrated.

During the dictatorship from November 1948 to January 1958, each of the Communist groups, as well as each of the other parties—Acción Democrática, Copei, and the Unión Republicana Democrática—controlled a small cluster of unions. There was no effective central labor organization in the country at that time, except for the puppet Confederación Nacional de Trabajadores established under government auspices during the last years of the dictatorship. The Communists and other party groups had no influence in the CNT, although a number of those who organized it for the government were former members of one or the other Communist party.

Apart from the 1936-44 period, Communist influence in organized labor was greatest from 1958 to 1961. During that span, the four parties with some following in organized labor formed a somewhat uneasy united front, and the Communists were able to acquire control of important union groups. They gained a large segment of the textile workers, the metal workers of Valencia, and a small number of petroleum workers' organizations. They also succeeded in getting extensive representation in the higher echelons of the labor movement, in the state and industrial federations, and in the reconstituted Confederación de Trabajadores de Venezuela.

Some idea of the strength of Communist influence in organized labor in the immediate post-Pérez Jiménez period can be gained from a report on the situation in the Federal District prepared by Eloy Torres on November 5, 1958, and contained in the Digepol Study.[7] The report is summarized in Table 4:

Table 4

PCV Infiltration in Unions
of Federal District

Secretary General a member of PCV	21
Additional PCV members in union directorate	17
PCV has influence but no directorate members	10
PCV has preponderant influence	19
Great PCV influence, sometimes decisive	16
PCV has some influence	9
PCV almost without influence	28

After the attempt of the Communists and the Movimiento de Izquierda Revolucionaria to convert the bank workers' strike of October-November 1960 into a revolutionary general walkout against the Betancourt government, the influence of the Communist Party in the ranks of organized labor steadily declined. During the period of urban terrorism and guerrilla war led by the Communist Party, it disappeared almost entirely.

The Communists were removed from top leadership positions in the labor movement soon after the events of November 1960. In the following year they suffered a setback in union elections throughout the country. Finally, well after the beginning of the terrorist campaign, the Communists and MIR felt so helpless in the Confederación de Trabajadores de Venezuela and its constituent organizations that they withdrew the trade unions under their control from the CTV. In April 1963, briefly joined by the few unions controlled by the Unión Republicana Democrática and the so-called ARS splinter from Acción Democrática, they formed a new labor group, the Central Unica de Trabajadores de Venezuela (CUTV). However, it is doubtful whether the CUTV ever had more than 10% of all organized labor in its ranks, and only part of this was under Communist control.

John D. Martz has commented thus on the attempt to establish the CUTV as a rival to the Acción Democrática-controlled Confederación de Trabajadores de Venezuela:[8]

> While the running battle with the CTV was increasingly articulated in terms of pro- or anti-government political declarations, the leadership of the CUTV began to crumble. What might have presented a substantial challenge to the CTV virtually collapsed as a result of inter-party rivalry within the CUTV leadership. . . . In early 1964 individual CUTV unions began to move over to the CTV, drawn by continual appeals for unity from Gonzalez Navarro. By May Day of 1964 the CTV's position was unchallengeable.

During the years of violence, Communist influence in the ranks of labor declined even further. Their principal leaders were jailed, including such trade union figures as Jesús Faria and Eloy Torres. Because the organized workers shared with most of the rest of the population a strong revulsion against the Communist resort to organized and continued violence, Communist leadership was removed from most of the unions they had still been able to control in 1963.

During the controversy within the party in 1965-67 over whether or not the Communists should withdraw from the guerrilla campaign, it was constantly reiterated that the Party had lost contact with the Venezuelan masses. Undoubtedly what had happened in the labor movement was a most important aspect of this general isolation from the rank and file citizenry, a concomitant of the Party's almost complete concentration on the use of violence.

The Communists have consistently sought influence in the peasant movement ever since it became an important political element during the first Acción Democrática government of 1945-58. However, their efforts in this field have been much less successful than their penetration of the organized urban labor movement.

Some information is available concerning the influence of the Communist Party in various peasant groups at a time (June 1961) when Communist influence in all sectors was perhaps at its peak. A report from the Digepol Study presents the following Communists claims:[9]

Table 5

Communist Strength in Peasant Groups

State	PCV-Controlled Peasant Groups	PCV-Influenced Peasant Groups	Total Peasant Groups
Lara	17	0	120
Portuguesa	16	12	172
Yaracuy	11	13	130
Trujillo	*	*	*
Miranda	16	0	120
Carabobo	16	0	60
Anzoátegui	4	4	*
Monagas	6	14	200
Aragua	16	*	*
Sucre	6	*	*
Zulia	4	*	*
Falcón	3	*	*

*No information given.

The report notes something of the nature of the Communists' efforts to penetrate the organized peasant movement:[10]

In the regions mentioned, except Falcón and Zulia, the PCV has 36 agrarian functionaries. Some of these are students, workers, and peasants who are given a one-week course before being sent to the countryside. Others will be sent. At least 250 will be sent during the vacations of August-September; some for a week, others for 15 days, and a few for 1-2 months. At the present time, 45 doctors of the PCV go to the countryside Saturdays and Sundays to examine the peasants and take medicines to them. Communist students of the faculties of agronomy also go. Brigades of teachers and theatrical groups are also being prepared. A plan of work is being elaborated which will be completed in December.

These data indicate that Communist influence among the peasantry was still small in 1961, but that the Party was then carrying on the type of varied activity which might have produced dividends, had it not the next year launched the all-out campaign of violence that alienated virtually the entire peasantry.

The one sector in which the Communists made progress in the 1958-62 period beyond that achieved in any previous period was the student sector, where, until the overthrow of the Pérez Jiménez dictatorship, they were a relatively small minority. Acción Democrática had been the majority political group among university students ever since the death of Juan Vicente Gómez.

Following the overthrow of the 1948-58 Pérez Jiménez dictatorship, the Communists emerged as the second most important political group among students. And although Acción Democrática still was first in numbers of adherents within the student body, the AD youth movement was in the extreme left wing of the party. Early in 1960 this group

185

split away from AD to form the Movimiento de Izquierda Revolucionaria. From then on, the student movement in the Central University of Caracas, by far the largest and most important in the country, was controlled by the MIR and PCV, who worked together. In several other universities, this extreme leftist coalition also prevailed.

The Communists and MIR recruited many, if not most, of the terrorists and guerrilla warriors in the 1962-66 period from university students. The grounds of the Central University were also used as headquarters for terrorists and guerrilla fighters and as an armory for those fighting to overthrow the regime.

However, once the PCV decided to withdraw from the guerrilla war, serious divergences began to develop between the Young Communists and the MIR followers in the universities. It is still too early to know whether these differences will be sufficient to destroy extreme leftist influence among the students.

As already mentioned, the Communists developed considerable influence after the fall of the Pérez Jiménez dictatorship among the residents of the shanty-town barrios on the hills above Caracas and in the suburbs of other cities. Until the resort to violence by the PCV and MIR in 1962, they were probably the two most popular political parties among these people. However, the campaign of violence also alienated most barrio dwellers, and by the time the Communists decided to withdraw from guerrilla activities in 1966, the PCV had lost virtually all the influence it had possessed in that segment of the population half a dozen years earlier. Time alone can tell whether the Communists will be able to rebuild their influence among this element by more pacific means.

In the period following the fall of Pérez Jiménez, the

Communists sought to organize "front groups" of various sorts, such as special women's organizations under party control. However, they had no marked success in this endeavor. Although they were able to bring into the Unión Nacional de Mujeres a few left-wing Acciondemocratistas, mainly those who had quit AD in 1960, they were able to establish only a handful of branch organizations in various parts of the country. One report reproduced in the Digepol Study indicated that while there were twenty-eight local committees of the UNM in the Federal District, only eighteen existed in the rest of the country, and state organizations of the Unión Nacional de Mujeres existed only in the states of Carabobo, Lara, Aragua, and Zulia.[11]

The Communists did succeed in establishing a "peace" organization which, under the leadership of retired General José R. Gabaldón, who was also a member of the international World Council of Peace, continued to function even after the Communists resorted to violence as the way to power. In 1965, this organization sent a message entitled "Document of Peace and Liberty" to the delegates at a meeting of the Organization of American States in Rio de Janeiro.[12] However, this particular group has not gained influence beyond the Communist Party and its close fellow travelers.

NONORGANIZATIONAL FRINGE GROUPS OF PCV

Unlike Communist groups in a number of other Latin American countries, the Communist Party in Venezuela has not been able to capitalize on the general Marxist-Leninist intellectual climate which undoubtedly exists there. Although Venezuelan intellectuals tend to accept the Marxist concept of the division of society into classes, and the Leninist picture of the world divided between imperialist nations and victims of imperialism, this has not produced an alliance of Venezuelan intellectuals with the Communist Party.

The reason is that political alternatives are available
to intellectuals, and to other important groups in Venezuelan society. Early in the modern history of Venezuela,
the Acción Democrática Party succeeded in bringing into
its ranks such leading literary figures as the poet Andrés
Eloy Blanco and the world-famous novelist Rómulo Gallegos. In the generations which came to maturity in the
1930's and 1940's, AD continued to attract most of the
intellectuals. A minority were also attracted to the Catholic social philosophy advocated by the Partido Copei.

However, since after the fall of the Pérez Jiménez
dictatorship, the Marxist-Leninist philosophy of the Partido Comunista de Venezuela and the Movimiento de Izquierda Revolucionaria had such a sizable following among university students, it is possible that in the next two or three
decades the generation schooled under their influence will
show a more marked attraction to the Marxist-Leninist
philosophy than their elders ever did.

POLITICAL COMPETITORS OF PCV

One of the keys to the fact that the Communist movement in Venezuela has never been a factor of major importance in the nation's political life is found in the political
groups with which it has had to compete. Primary among
these is Acción Democrática, but others have also been
of some importance, including Copei, Unión Republica
Democrática, the Frente Democrático Popular, Movimiento
de Izquierda Revolucionaria, and even the Frente Nacional
Democrático of Arturo Uslar Pietri.

Acción Democrática has been the largest party in
Venezuela for more than a quarter of a century. It is a
party that grew out of the struggle against the Gómez and
López Contreras dictatorships, and it is headed by an ex-
Communist (Rómulo Betancourt).

Acción Democrática has developed an ideology or philosophy and a program which much of the population apparently feels is peculiarly adapted to the Venezuelan milieu. From the beginning it has proclaimed itself a multi-class party, seeking to represent the interests of the urban workers, the peasantry, and the middle class. It has from the earliest days advocated agrarian reform—redistribution of the country's landholdings to the advantage of landless peasants and those agriculturalists with too little land to provide an adequate living; labor and social legislation; and making education, medical facilities, and other elements of modern civilization available to the great bulk of the population.

Acción Democrática has also been consistently a nationalist party. This aspect of its program is best expressed in its attitude toward the petroleum industry. Since the early 1940's it has opposed granting new concessions to foreign oil companies, and has advocated the eventual transfer of the oil industry to national ownership. It has urged that pending such transfer, the Venezuelan government insist on getting the greatest possible economic and financial benefit from any exploitation of its oil resources, and that the proceeds from the oil industry be used for the purpose of diversifying the national economy and raising the people's living standards.

Finally, Acción Democrática has consistently affirmed its faith in the democratic form of government and in the democratic organization of Venezuelan society. Born out of protest to the López Contrera dictatorship, it has opposed every dictatorial regime since then. It has had more martyrs than all other political parties in Venezuela since the late 1930's. Even more important, when in power Acción Democrática has governed according to democratic principles.

However, it has not been only Acción Democrática's announced program which has appealed to a large segment of the Venezuelan populace. During its two periods in power, AD has moved energetically to carry out the program it has advocated. AD has put into effect a widespread agrarian reform, it has vastly expanded the educational system, it has brought schools, sewers, water supplies, electricity, paved streets, and adequate housing to large segments of the interior population which never before had them. Its policy has been nationalist, not only in terms of petroleum, but of industrialization and of foreign policy.

Hence, Acción Democrática has constituted the single largest roadblock to the advance of the Communists. Since it first won the major part of the labor movement in 1944, AD has kept this control, and since the peasant movement was established during the first Acción Democrática regime of 1945-48, AD has completely dominated it. Intellectuals and professional people have also given AD wide support. Since 1959 it has even been accepted by elements of the upper classes, particularly the industrialists, and by large segments of the armed forces, both of whom approve its economic development efforts, its ability to provide a relatively stable government, and its democratic regime.

However, for all its past successes, there are some stormclouds visible on the AD horizon. The position of Acción Democrática in the Venezuelan political system has been seriously weakened by a party split which occurred late in 1967. As a result of long-standing internal feuds which climaxed in the struggle over who should be the AD nominee in the 1968 presidential election, a large segment of Acción Democrática has broken away under the titular leadership of Luis Beltrán Prieto Figueroa, and the political direction of AD's former secretary general, Jesús Paz Galarraga.

The Prieto-Paz Galarraga group, under the name Movimiento de Educación Popular, has organized as a party separate from Acción Democrática. As a result, Luis Beltrán Prieto became the 1968 MEP candidate for president, in competition with Gonzalo Barrios, nominee of the orthodox Acción Democrática, and candidates put in the field by various other parties. For electoral purposes, the MEP made an alliance with the PRIN, consisting largely of former AD members who separated from the party in the MIR and ARS splits of 1960 and 1962.

Because of the large number of leaders and rank-and-file members of Acción Democrática who joined the MEP schism, the party's position as the dominant element in Venezuelan politics is seriously endangered. As this is being written (in September 1968), it is too early to know what the lasting importance of the split will be and to what degree it will facilitate Communist attempts to gain supporters among the country's workers and peasants.

In recent years, the principal party rival of Acción Democrática has been Copei, Venezuela's Christian Democratic organization. Although Copei tended to be fairly conservative during its early years, i.e., during AD's first period in power in 1945-48, it emerged as a party of the democratic Left after the overthrow of Pérez Jiménez. Between 1959 and 1964 it participated in the Betancourt coalition government with Acción Democrática, and helped to carry out that government's program of social reform and economic development. Lately, it has developed some influence both in the organized labor movement and among the peasants. It is fairly strong among the middle class, and is the party most favored by the Church. It also has a certain degree of support among the officer class of the armed forces.

The Copei has therefore presented a realistic democratic alternative to Acción Democrática. Since the election of 1963, in which it emerged as the country's second largest party, its leaders have been convinced that their party will win power, if not in the 1968 election, at least in 1973.[*] Because of this expectation and the party's firm commitment to political democracy, Copei has since 1964 offered Venzuela an experience it has never had before: since the inception of the Leoni government, Copei has served as the "loyal opposition." Although critical of the Leoni government, it has been unwilling to resort to any means outside the rules of democratic politics to oust that regime. Never before has Venezuela had such an opposition; always in the past, coup d'etat has been accepted as the "normal" way to get rid of a government in power. Thus, since 1964 Copei, as the major opposition party, has done at least as much to strengthen the position of democratic government in Venzuela as it did during the Betancourt government, when it shared the responsibilities of administration.

Unión Republicana Democrática has also been an important rival to the Communist Party. Since 1958 URD has been a more or less democratic opponent of AD on the Left. Although the ideology of the URD is somewhat indefinite and has tended to shift with the political winds, the party has never since 1959 seriously contemplated any but democratic means to oust the AD from power. During the Leoni government it was a partner in the administration, a fact which probably tended to strengthen its devo-- tion to the democratic way.

---

[*] Since this text was written, the Copei won the 1968 presidential election, Rafael Caldera gaining less than 1 percent more than AD candidate Gonzolo Barrios. Caldera was inaugurated in March 1969.

AD, Copei, and the URD have been the country's largest parties since 1945. However, a few other groups which have appeared since 1958 have also constituted blocks to the extension of Communist influence, because they have tended to siphon off some of the opposition to Acción Democrática which might otherwise have found its way into the ranks, or at least the periphery, of the Partido Comunista de Venezuela.

One of these minor groups is the Frente Democrático Popular, better known as the party of Admiral Wolfgang Larrazábal. Although the Admiral has symbolized this party since its foundation in the last years of the Betancourt regime, its moving political force has been Jorge Dáger, a one-time Acciondemocratista who was briefly a member of MIR, but who quit that party when it decided to take the violent road to power. Admiral Wolfgang Larrazábal and his party have continued to figure in national politics, and have appealed particularly to the barrio dwellers. They have undoubtedly presented a democratic alternative to Acción Democrátic for many in the shantytowns of Caracas who might otherwise have followed the Communists in their experiment with urban terrorism.

The PRIN is another left-wing rival of Acción Democrática that has to some degree weakened the Communists. This group was first organized as the Acción Democrática-Oposición, when the so-called ARS group broke away from AD in December 1961. After the election of 1936, in which the ARS did badly, it took the name Partido Revolucionario Nacionalista. Subsequently, after Domingo Alberto Rangel and his followers had left the MIR in 1965 over the issue of continuing the campaign of violence against the Leoni government, the PRN merged with the Rangel group and with a left-wing element of the Unión Republicana Democrática which had been expelled from that party in December 1963. The new group that emerged was the Partido Revolucionario de la Izquierda Nacionalista (PRIN).

The PRIN is important because it is the most left-wing of the legal parties in opposition to the Leoni government. It has presented an alternative within the constitutional system for those who may have agreed with the Communists' condemnation of the Acción Democrática regime, but disagreed with the Communists' decision to try to overthrow that government by force.

Of some importance, too, as a block to the Communists since 1963 has been the Frente Nacional Democrático. This is the party organized by Arturo Uslar Pietri who, as an independent candidate for the presidency in the 1963 election, came in fourth. The FND has rallied many conservative elements critical of the Acción Democrática regime. It also has considerable strength, on the basis of Uslar Pietri's own personal popularity, among the barrio dwellers, and so has given many of them an alternative to the Communists.

Finally, even the Movimiento de Izquierda Revolucionaria has helped to bar the progress of the Communist Party. Like the Communists, it has claimed to be Marxist-Leninist in ideology. It has pictured itself as being left of the Communists, and in recent months has proved this to be the case. It has been the single largest element among the students, particularly those of the Central University of Caracas, and has thus diverted supporters who, had it not existed, would probably have been attracted to the Communist Party.

Thus, a major roadblock to Communist progress in Venezuela has been the competition it has faced from other parties. Som of these have been recognizably to the right of the Communists, others to the left. However, each has had a special appeal to one or more groups to which the Communists have over the years tried to appeal. Some of them, especially Acción Democrática and Copei, have presented the possibility of actually accomplishing within a relatively short time the goals, such as agrarian reform, rapid industrialization, a nationalistic oil policy, and labor and social legislation, which the Communists have been able to promise only as long-range objectives.

The existence of this multitude of parties, all of some importance in the national political picture, has had the further effect of preventing Venezuelan politics from becoming polarized, as has occurred in some other Latin American countries. The citizens of Venezuela have never been presented with the Communists as the only alternative to a political group opposed by a large part of the population. The people have had a number of alternatives, most of them within the democratic constitutional framework, at least one outside the law.

CURRENT STRATEGY OF PCV

During the period 1962-66, when it was concentrating on the violent road to power, the Partido Comunista de Venezuela virtually abandoned the political stage to its various rivals. However, in 1966 it decided to renounce the guerrilla war strategy it was then following, and to attempt to compete with other parties for the support of the Venezuelan masses.

As the instrument for this repenetration of the masses, the Communists established early in 1968 the Unión Para Avanzar (UPA). It was given legal recognition as a political party, although its principal officials were leaders of the Communist Party.

Soon after his release from jail in May 1968, Gustavo Machado defined the immediate objectives the UPA was seeking when he said: "For now, we aspire to name lists of candidates, so that we can have our representatives in the Congress, the legislative assemblies and the municipal councils. " Machado immediately undertook a nationwide tour to reestablish the party's organizations in various parts of the country. Meanwhile, Gonzalo Barrios, official presidential candidate of the Acción Democrática Party, announced that, if they wished to do so, the Unión Para Avanzar would be perfectly free to name Gustavo Machado as its nominee for president. [13]

Participation in the electoral campaign of 1968 can undoubtedly be valuable to the Communists in rehabilitating their political reputation, and in putting them once again in contact with the masses. It may become a means by which the Communists will regain some influence in the labor and peasant movements.

However, there remain indications that the Venezuelan Communists do not reject categorically a future recourse to violence. Thus, Teodoro Petkoff, in Problemas de la Paz y del Socialismo, the pro-Moscow international Communist periodical published in Bogotá, Colombia, wrote in its issue No. 116 of 1968, "As part of a general policy which seeks to accent today the political offensive, with the temporary suspension of military operations, we are undergoing reorganization, reenforcing our cadres, but our criterion has not varied. For us the armed struggle is a fundamental way to power in Venezuela, and any democratic or revolutionary change must be associated necessarily with the armed struggle. . . . "[14]

Chapter Six

PCV RELATIONS WITH OTHER COMMUNIST PARTIES

The relationships of the Venezuelan Communist Party with its counterparts in other parts of the world, particularly with those in power, have been of major importance in the evolution of the PCV. For a long period, spanning virtually its entire history, the PCV's contact with the Communist Party of the Soviet Union was the lodestar of its behavior. For the relatively short period between 1962 and 1966, relations with the ruling Communist Party of Cuba were of key significance. Its connections with the pre-Castro Communist Party of Cuba, and with the parties of the United States, China, and Italy are less important, but worthy of menion.

RELATIONS WITH CPSU

From its inception, the Communist Party of Venezuela has had close relations with the Communist Party of the Soviet Union. One of the PCV's principal founders, Ricardo Martínez, was an official of the Communist International, living in Moscow, even before the Venezuelan party was officially established.

In 1935 the Venezuelan Party joined the Communist International as a full-fledged national section. It consistently followed the "line" of the International, as laid down by the CPSU, from then until the breakup of the Communist monolith in the late 1950's or early 1960's. During the 1939-41 period, when the Soviet Union was an ally of Nazi Germany, the Venezuelan Communist Party could find nothing to choose between the Allies and the Axis. When the Soviet Union was invaded by Germany, the Venezuelan Communist Party became an enthusiastic supporter of the Allied cause. After the War, the Venezuelan Party reflected the growing hostility of the Soviet Union toward the United States by finding that the United States had taken the place of Nazi Germany as "the principal enemy of the working class. "

Unlike some other Latin American Communist parties, the PCV has experienced no drastic intervention by the Comintern or the Communist Party of the Soviet Union to overturn its leadership, although in the 1930's the Comintern did on occasion expel individual leaders of the PCV. Likewise, the Soviet leadership indirectly endorsed the "Red" Communist party as "official"after the Unity Congress of November 1946, at which this group was organized, in preference to the rival "Black" party, the Partido Revolucionario Proletario (Comunista).

During the 1950's the Communists of Venezuela continued to follow the line of the international Communist movement, oriented primarily toward Moscow. In its underground and exile publications, for example, it carried on the "peace" campaigns associated with the so-called "Stockholm Peace Petition. " Representatives of both the "Red" and "Black" Communist groups took part in the activities of the Moscow-controlled World Federation of Trade Unions.

Throughout their history, the Venezuelan Communists have held up the Soviet Union as the model of what they are trying to achieve in their own country, and have proclaimed their loyalty to the Soviet Union. For example, the periodical of the "Black" Communists, P. R. P. Comunista, in its issue of March 12, 1948, ran an article on the first page entitled "Por Qué Estamos Con la Unión Sovietica" (Why We Are with the Soviet Union). This article read in part:

> The choice between the two worlds is not difficult to make: the exploiters, the usurpers of the means of production and their 'lackeys' coalesce to defend and maintain the capitalist world. The workers, laborers and peasants, the middle classes bind ever tighter from country to country the fraternal bonds of struggle for unitedly winning their socialist world. The Soviet Union, in hurling back the Nazi-Fascist hordes not only saved humanity from return to barbarism which was represented by the triumph of Hitler, but assured for all humanity the advent within a short time of the socialist world. . . .

> The peoples of the Soviet Union, with their imperishable heroism of October 1917, in the years of allied military occupation, in the period of pacific construction and then in Stalingrad, Leningrad, Moscow, Berlin, have conquered the socialist world of humanity. Most advanced of all the peoples, our enemies are your enemies. To destroy us and keep us enslaved and in servitude, they want to destroy you. Defending ourselves, we defend you. Defending yourselves, you defend us.

Thirteen years later, the reunited Partido Comunista de Venezuela issued the pamphlet by Guillermo García Ponce, Introducción a la Política Venezolana, which served as a basis for study in various levels of party schools. Here, too, the Soviet Union is cited as the model. In discussing the "character of the State," García Ponce writes:[1]

The character of the State is determined by its
class content. By the social classes which have
in their hands its instruments and institutions.

For example: the United States is a capitalist
country. Its dominant social class is the class
of the capitalists. The State is in the hands of
these capitalists; then, the State has a capitalist
character.

The Soviet Union is a socialist country. The
dominant class is the working class. The State
is in the hands of the workers. The Socialist
State has a proletarian class character.

During the early 1960's the Venezuelan Communist
Party passed through what was probably the most difficult
period in its relations with the CPSU, when it was attempting to seize power through urban terrorism and guerrilla
warfare, a line of action not particularly favored by the
Soviet party insofar as Latin America in general was concerned. However, the PCV succeeded in maintaining
good relations with the CPSU during this period, as demonstrated by the fact that World Marxist Review, the organ
of the pro-Soviet group of Communist parties, carried
regular and fairly extensive reports on the PCV's activities.

It seems probable that the Communist Party of the
Soviet Union threw its weight on the side of withdrawal
from the guerrilla war when the PCV made this decision
in 1966-67. When Jesús Faria, PCV Secretary General,
was released from prison by the Leoni government, he
headed straight for Moscow, and was reported to have
been met at the airport there by high Soviet party officials.
Faria was a leading advocate within the PCV of withdrawal from the experiment with violence and of return

to mass work in trade unions and other groups.

RELATIONS WITH THE CASTRO PARTY

The Communist Party of Cuba, led by Secretary General Fidel Castro, has influenced the PCV even more than that of the Soviet Union in recent years. Cuba was most influential in committing the PCV to a policy of violence in 1962, and the party's decision to cease that campaign in 1966 brought down upon it the full vehemence of Fidel's wrath.

With the victory of the Castro revolution in January 1959, the PCV and most other political groups in Venezuela, and other Communist parties throughout Latin America, threw their support strongly behind the new Cuban regime. Although the Castro government was by no means Communist at that time, the Venezuelan Communists carried out extensive propaganda on its behalf. Delegations sent to Cuba included young people who received "training" of various kinds early in the Castro period.

As the Castro regime moved closer to the Cuban Communists, and finally declared itself to be part of "the Socialist camp" in world affairs in December 1961, it lost the support of virtually all non-Communist elements in Venezuelan politics, but the enthusiasm of the Partido Comunista de Venezuela for the Cuban Revolution became even more intense. This trend was already evident in Jesús Faria's Report to the Third Congress of the PCV in March 1961:[2]

> The example of Cuba has raised to a higher level the consciousness of the Latin American masses. The Declaration of Havana expresses not only the aspirations of the people of Cuba, but also those of all the peoples of Latin America. . . . The

Declaration of Havana and the accomplishments
of the Government of Cuba are the political and
social revolution speaking Spanish, carried out
not in the distant lands of Asia or Europe, but
right here, in the Caribbean, a few miles from
the United States, within the family of peoples
and countries oppressed by the voracious imperialist monopolists. For this reason, it is
correct that the Cuban revolution be defended as
something which is very much ours. In the
degree that the hostility of its enemies and their
lackeys in our countries increases, there must
also increase the solidarity of our peoples toward
that revolution and its accomplishments.

With the outbreak of violence in Venezuela, spear-
headed by the Partido Comunista de Venezuela and the
Movimiento de Izquierda Revolucionaria, the Cuban party
and government made no secret of their support. Through
the so-called Fuerzas Armadas de Liberación Nacional,
they supplied funds, arms, training facilities, and personnel to the urban terrorists and the rural guerrillas under
the direction of the PCV and MIR.

The reversal in policy in 1966-67 brought the PCV
into sharp conflict with the Communist Party of Cuba.
Castro himself launched the clash on March 13, 1967, during a speech commemorating the tenth anniversary of an
attack by revolutionaries on the presidential palace of
Fulgencio Batista. Most of his speech was devoted to the
situation in Venezuela. Castro traced the details of the
change in the PCV's attitude toward guerrilla activity, and
denounced by name Pompeyo Márquez, Teodoro Petkoff,
Freddy Muñoz, and Guillermo García Ponce, all of whom
had urged the Communist Party of Venezuela to "under-
take a retrenchment on the military front and recommend
the suspension of armed actions in favor of proceeding to

a regrouping of its forces and their preparation for a new revolutionary stage. . . ."

Castro proclaimed his support for Douglas Bravo and other guerrilla leaders who were continuing the armed effort. Bravo had been suspended from membership in the Political Bureau of the Communist Party of Venezuela and soon afterward was expelled from the party for his insistence on going ahead with the violence. Castro repudiated the leadership of the Venezuelan Communist Party, which had disciplined Bravo, in the following terms:[3]

No one who claims to call himself Communist will support the rightist official leadership opposing Douglas Bravo. Communist parties must differentiate between the guerrillas who are fighting in Venezuela and the defeatists who wish to renounce the struggle, who in practice wish to give up the guerrilla movement. And this will be a dividing line, for we are arriving at the time of definitions, not by anyone's whims, but by the force of the process itself, of historical events themselves.

The Venezuelan Communist Party leadership lost no time in replying to Castro. On March 15, 1967 they issued a denunciation of the Cuban leader, in the name of the Political Bureau of the Communist Party of Venezuela, signed by Pompeyo Márquez, Guillermo García Ponce, Alonso Ojeda Oleache, Pedro Ortega Díaz, Eduardo Gallegos Mancera, Teodoro Petkoff, and Germán Lairet. In this strongly worded statement, the Venezuelan Communist leadership accused Castro of "an irresponsible arrogance and self-sufficiency which are improper in a Chief of State." It then went on to make four major points. The first was that although the Venezuelan Communists admired the Cuban revolution and looked to it for inspiration and guidance, "we are not and we shall never be agents of Cuba in Venezuela, as we are not agents of any other Communist Party in the world. We are Venezuelan Communists and we do not admit tutelage from anyone, no matter how great his revolutionary merits may be."

The second point was a denial of Fidel's charge that the Venezuelan Communist leaders were "cowards." They commented that his accusation was "a new demonstration of that irritating tendency of his to believe himself to have a monopoly of valor and courage," and added that "the Venezuelan Communists are not possessed of the puerile exhibitionism to proclaim their qualities in this field." However, they went on to recite various examples of Venezuelan Communist courage, from Gustavo Machado's invasion of the country from Curacao in 1929 down to the most recent guerrilla activities in which the party had participated.

They then denounced Castro for assuming "once again the role of a kind of arbiter of the revolutionary destinies of Latin America, and of a super-revolutionary who in contrast to all of the Communists of Latin America has already made the revolution." They added, ". . . we wish to reject the role of revolutionary 'Pope' which Fidel Castro has arrogated to himself. We categorically reject his pretension that it should be he and no one else but he who decides what is or is not revolutionary in Latin America."

Finally, the Venezuelan Communists noted, "this is a disagreeable polemic and undoubtedly will please the enemy," but added "evidently it is now unpostponable. We have come to the limit, where Fidel Castro himself obliges us to answer. . . . We will not tolerate in anyone the insolent and provocative language which he used in his speech of March 13."[4]

The feud with the Cuban Communist leadership continued after this exchange of compliments in March 1967. In May of that year, when Cuban army officers were among a group of would-be guerrillas caught after landing on the Venezuelan coast, the Communist Party of Venezuela announced its opposition to this interference in Venezuelan internal affairs. The New York Times of May 18, 1967 reported as follows on this incident:

> The CP Central Committee, in a move to dissociate itself from the evidence of Cuban intervention, published today paid newspaper advertisements denouncing the "insurrectional line" being followed by Cuban-backed guerrillas.

> In its statement today, the Moscow-oriented CP said that "at this moment the armed movement does not have the capacity to play a decisive role because of the stagnation of the guerrilla fronts."

> The Central Committee said the correct line instead of insurrection—either through guerrillas or urban terrorism—was to join forces with other progressive political elements in a "popular front" movement in support of an opposition candidate for President next year.

> "We have decided to participate in elections, suspend armed operations and put the emphasis on a policy of broad alliance to regroup the democratic opposition" the party statement said.

In July 1967 delegates from the PCV were noticably absent from the founding congress of the Organización Latino Americana de Solidaridad (OLAS) in Havana; they had quite pointedly not been invited to send representatives to the meeting. Furthermore, this OLAS congress, engineered and run by the Communist Party of Cuba, formally denounced the Partido Comunista de Venezuela. A resolution, which passed by fifteen votes to three, condemned "the bungling, opportunist position of the rightist leadership of the Venezuelan CP, which by abandoning the road of armed struggle betrayed revolutionary principles and is serving the interests of imperialism and the oligarchies and all their policies of oppression."[5]

Fidel Castro himself used this congress as a platform to attack once again the PCV leadership. The tone of his attack can be judged from the following paragraphs:[6]

> This Party, or rather the rightist leadership of
> the Venezuelan Party, has come to adopt a posi-
> tion which smacks of an enemy of revolutionaries,
> an instrument of imperialism and the oligarchy.
> And I do not say this for the sake of talking; I
> am not a slanderer, I am not a defamer.

> We have some unfinished business with that group
> of traitors. We have not encouraged polemics;
> we have not incited conflicts; far from that, for
> a long time we have kept silent while enduring a
> barrage of documents and attacks from that right-
> ist leadership, as that leadership forsook the
> guerrilla fighters and took the road of concilia-
> tion and submission.

He accused the PCV leaders of "deceit" in their maneuvering to get out of the guerrilla war. Throughout much of the speech he refers to the PCV leadership and other groups in sympathy with it as "The Mafia."

RELATIONS WITH OTHER COMMUNIST PARTIES

The Venezuelan Communists have also had contacts

with other national Communist groups over the years. During the late 1930's and through at least the first half of the 1940's, relations with the Communist Party of the United States were of considerable significance. An American Communist, then working as an agent of the Communist International, Joseph Kornfedder, was present at the founding congress of the Partido Comunista de Venezuela in 1931.[7] A few years later, during the Seventh Congress of the Comintern in 1935, the CPUSA was given a special role in supervising the activities of several Latin American Communist parties, particularly those in nations bordering the Caribbean.[8]

The close relationship of the United States party with various Latin American parties continued throughout the remainder of Earl Browder's leadership of the CPUSA and for some time thereafter. Thus, a representative of the United States party was present at the Unity Congress which gave rise to the "Red" party, the Partido Comunista de Venezuela, in 1946. A letter from William Z. Foster, then President of the Communist Party of the United States, gave the imprimatur of orthodoxy to the group which emerged from the Unity Congress. Foster's letter, which was addressed to the Central Committee of the Partido Comunista de Venezuela and its three-man secretariat, was widely published in Communist and pro-Communist publications throughout Latin America, among them, for instance, Vicente Lombardo Toledano's daily newspaper El Popular in Mexico City, and the Cuban party's "theoretical" journal, Fundamentos. The letter referred to "the historical conquest signified by having obtained a unified Communist movement in Venezuela," and added, "I and my comrades have followed with great interest the final consolidation of unity among the Venezuelan Communists last November and the important work which your deputies Juan Bautista Fuenmayor and Gustavo Machado are carrying out in the Venezuelan National Constituent

Assembly." Foster concluded: "I send a handshake of
solidarity to your united Party and its new working class
leadership. I wish you success in your struggles to safeguard the independence of your country and for democratic
progress there."9

The pre-Castro Cuban Communist Party, known as
the Partido Socialista Popular, also was involved in the
internal affairs of the Venezuelan Communist movement.
Cuban delegates played a significant role in the Unity Congress of 1946, at a time when the Cuban party was closely
associated with the CPUSA in supervising activities of
Communist parties in the Caribbean area. 10

After the Chinese Communist Party came to power,
the PCV joined others in hailing their victory and in citing
the Chinese party as a prime example of a Communist
party in power. An example of this enthusiasm for the
Chinese party is a pamphlet which the "Red" party published in the early 1950's in connection with its trade union
training school, the Escuela Sindical Ezequiel Zamora.
This pamphlet reprinted several articles, including one
from the World Federation of Trade Unions periodical
El Movimiento Sindical Mundial which dealt at considerable length with the role of trade unions in Communist
China. 11

Once the split between the Chinese Communists and
the CPSU became open, the Venezuelan party held to a
more or less neutral position. It attempted to maintain
good relations with both parties, and the fact that it succeeded in doing so, at least so long as it was engaged in
its campaigns of violence in the early 1960's, was demonstrated by the fact that both World Marxist Review, the
organ of the pro-Moscow parties, and Peking Review, a
major international publication of the Chinese, continued
to carry articles about and favorable references to the

Venezuelan Party and its activities. Some Venezuelan Communists, including Politburo member Eduardo Gallegos Mancera, visited China during this period.

However, the situation of the PCV in the world-wide factional struggle within the Communist movement changed substantially after 1967 when the party abandoned, at least temporarily, its attempt to come to power by force. As we have indicated, this decision was probably encouraged by the Russians, violently opposed by the Cubans, and presumably also dimly viewed by the Chinese.

In their reply to Fidel Castro's diatribe against them in March 1967, the Venezuelan Communists endorsed, insofar as it applied to them, the idea of "polycentrism," that is, their right to run their own affairs without interference from outside Venezuela. The PCV Political Bureau's reply to Castro said: "The PCV insists upon its right to lay down its own policy, without interference from anyone." Later they added the statement we have already quoted: "We are Venezuelan Communists, and do not admit tutelage from anyone no matter how great may be his revolutionary merits."[12]

Finally, the relationship of the Italian Communist Party to the PCV during the guerrilla period should be mentioned. On April 10, 1965 Minister of Interior Gonzalo Barrios announced the arrest of three foreigners who had brought $330,000 from Italy to finance Communist terrorism in Venezuela. He described the three as money carriers for the Italian Communist Party, which had been designated the "contact organization" with Latin America at a meeting of European Communist parties in the Soviet Union. The money had come from the USSR. Those arrested were Mrs. Clara Ava Baretic de Padilla, a 32-year-old Argentine of Yugoslav origin; Alejandro Beltramini, 54, an Italian surgeon and Communist member of the Milan city council; and Mrs. Josefa Ventosa Jiménez, 22, a Spaniard who had spent some time in East Germany and Czechoslovakia. [13]

CONCLUSION

During the decades when the international Communist movement was more or less monolithic and directed from Moscow, the PCV was subjected to supervision by the CPSU through the Comintern and, later, the Cominform. However, in the 1930's and 1940's the Communist parties of the United States and of Cuba cooperated in the orientation of the Venezuelan movement, and of various others in Latin America.

With the advent of the schism between the Soviet Union and China, and with the added complication of the Castro party's bid for hemispheric leadership, the Venezuelan party attempted at first to maintain friendly relations with all contending factions. It succeeded so long as it was engaged in the attempt to seize power by force, even though this strategy lacked the wholehearted approval of the CPSU. However, the 1966-67 withdrawal of the PCV from guerrilla activities opened a scission with the Partido Comunista de Cuba under Castro's leadership, and presumably also worsened relations with the Chinese Communists, especially since the CPSU gave the Venezuelans advice on the subject of their about-face.

Chapter Seven

PRINCIPAL DETERMINANTS OF PCV BEHAVIOR

Four factors have primarily determined the behavior of the Communist movement in Venezuela. Three of these are national in nature, originating within Venezuela; the fourth influence comes from abroad. All four factors are interrelated, but for purposes of analysis they can be differentiated as follows: the frequency of dictatorships; the type of political competition the Communists have encountered; pressures from within the Venezuelan Communist ranks; and finally, the influence of foreign Communist parties, particularly those of the Soviet Union and Cuba.

INFLUENCE OF DICTATORSHIPS

The dictatorships that have prevailed during long periods of recent Venezuelan history have had a significant impact on the Venezuelan Communist Party. They have forced the Communists to function underground for years at a time—from 1937 to 1941, from 1950 to 1958.

The need to operate thus illegally has affected the Communists in various ways. For one thing, their illegality made them smaller in number, and perhaps more tightly knit, than in the more democratic epochs.

But the dictatorships, particularly that of 1948-58, have also engendered controversy within the Communists' ranks regarding policies to be followed toward the regime. Thus, in the early years of the 1948-58 dictatorship, the "Red" Communists followed a policy of strong opposition to the military regime, whereas the "Blacks" made their peace with it and in fact collaborated with it to a considerable degree. Also, even among the Reds, controversy over the nature and degree of opposition resulted in the purge of Juan Bautista Fuenmayor and other important leaders from the party in 1951.

The need to operate illegally during the dictatorial periods also hampered the Communists' work with the masses. Such organizations as trade unions and peasant groups either did not function at all during these periods, or were severely crippled, and in any case did not have great masses of people in their ranks. Thus the Communists were severely limited in one of their important recruiting fields. They also had much more difficulty during these periods organizing front groups on particular issues.

However, in one sense at least, the dictatorships, particularly that between November 1948 and January 1958, gave the Communists a kind of opportunity they did not normally have during more democratic times. In the name of "unity in the struggle against the dictatorship" they could approach other, normally hostile, parties, and offer a united front. This appeal inevitably had a certain popularity among other parties which were being persecuted by the regime, and which were anxious to avoid weakening the struggle against it by bitter inter-party quarrels among opponents of the dictatorship.

Although the Communists' calls for united action with other parties, particularly with Acción Democrática, were never accepted by the exiled leaders of these groups or by older leaders of the underground, they did appeal to younger underground leaders, especially of Acción Democrática, during the last years of the struggle against Pérez Jiménez. Thus the underground of the three other parties—AD, Copei and Unión Republicana Democrática—did work closely with the Communists during the last year of the Pérez Jiménez dictatorship. Also, the Acción Democrática Youth, and some younger leaders and members of the URD, emerged from the dictatorship with a strong feeling of solidarity and comradeship for the Communists. In the years that followed, this resulted in serious defections from the AD, and led in 1960 to the formation of the Movimiento de Izquierda Revolucionaria, and to less significant splits in Unión Republicana Democrática.

POLITICAL COMPETITION

The political competition faced by the Communist movement of Venezuela has been an important determinant of its behavior. Throughout virtually its entire existence, another party on the Left, AD, has appealed to exactly the same groups, has promised many of the same short-run achievements, and has had the advantage of seeming more likely to fulfill its promises within a relatively short time than the Communists.

Acción Democrática has been the chief rival of the Communists in the ranks of organized labor, in the peasant movement, even in some middle-class organizations. In recent years, Copei also has developed some following here.

Acción Democrática's program has appealed to the desire of large numbers of Venezuelans for basic social reforms, rapid economic development, and more independent handling of the country's international relations. In addition, its leadership, headed by Rómulo Betancourt, has been widely popular and has maintained the loyalty of wide segments of workers, peasants, and the intelligentsia through several decades of good times and bad, through lengthy periods in power and through even longer periods of being outlawed and persecuted by dictatorial regimes.

Finally, Acción Democrática has had by far the best and most extensive political organization of any party in Venezuela. Established by Betancourt and others in the late 1930's and kept intact ever since, AD organization extends to all parts of the country; in 1963 nearly one million Venezuelans belonged to Acción Democrática. During democratic periods, members have been kept active in direct party work and within other groups, such as unions and peasant groups. Large numbers, too, have passed through training schools and courses maintained by the party, which has strengthened their knowledge of party doctrine and of AD tactics and strategy. Finally, in contrast to the situation in the Communist Party, rank and file members of AD and local leaders participate in important party decision.

How to deal with Acción Democrática has always been a major subject of controversy within Communist ranks. Except for a short period in the late 1950's, when young and inexperienced leaders of the AD underground, cut off from older leaders, developed sympathy for the Communists, Acción Democrática has been virtually impervious to Communist blandishments. Nevertheless, one school of thought within Communist ranks has favored attempts to form an alliance with AD, the country's major popular party and therefore potentially the most profitable PCV recruiting ground; other elements have generally opposed the idea of making any overtures to Acción Democrática. These attitudes conduced toward the split in the party's ranks in the early 1940's which persisted for at least a decade.

In recent years Copei, the country's Christian Democratic or Catholic Social party, has also developed some influence in mass organizations. Smaller than AD, it too has had capable leadership and a capacity for intensive organizational work, through which it has succeeded since 1958 in establishing itself throughout Venezuela. Although sentiment within the Communist Party has not favored formation of a united front with Copei, the rise of Copei has handicapped the Communists in presenting a democratic alternative to Acción Democrática to workers, peasants, or intellectuals who had become disillusioned with that party.

The existence of AD and Copei has prevented Venezuelan politics from becoming polarized as in Chile, for instance, where the alternative for several decades has been principally between the Communists and their allies, and those who are strongly opposed to the Communists. In Venezuela, except when they resorted to violence in the 1960's, the Communists have never been a major factor or issue in national politics.

Many Communists have often seen the best tactic as trying to form some kind of alliance with the Unión Republicana Democrática. The last of the "big three" of Venezuelan politics, the URD has differed from AD and Copei in lacking a well-defined ideology. It has been led by politicians whose qualities have included a high degree of tactical "versatility," which some call opportunism. Finally, it has been less tightly knit and less disciplined than the other two parties.

The PCV sought an alliance with URD in the election of 1958, when both PCV and URD supported the presidential candidacy of Admiral Wolfgang Larrazábal. Subsequently, when URD joined the Betancourt government, the PCV did not attack URD with the vehemence it used to denounce URD's coalition partners, AD and Copei, and sought to get URD to withdraw from the coalition—which URD did in November 1960. Still later, the PCV attempted to maintain good relations with Unión Republicana Democrática even while engaging in its violent campaign to overthrow the Betancourt government, a campaign the URD supposedly did not approve. Undoubtedly some contacts were maintained between PCV and URD leaders during this period.

A number of small parties on the Left have developed during the 1960's. The most important of these have been the Frente Democrático Popular of Admiral Larrazábal and Jorge Dager, and the Partido Revolucionario de la Izquierda Nacionalista, formed in 1965 by a merger of the old ARS dissidents from Acción Democrática, the Domingo Alberto Rangel peaceful faction of the MIR, and a left-wing group which had been expelled from URD in 1963.

During its resort to violence, the PCV tried to maintain friendly relations with the small left-wing groups, although internal Communist Party documents indicate that the attitude toward these parties was in fact one of disdain. They were frequently referred to as "collaborationists," meaning that they cooperated with the regime which the PCV was trying to overthrow.

These parties took on new significance for the Partido Comunista de Venezuela subsequent to its decision to withdraw from violence and seek contacts with "the masses" once again. The element of the masses ideologically nearest to the Communists and therefore most likely to be receptive to their overtures was these small Leftist parties, which were, like the Communists, in opposition.

Finally, Movimiento de Izquierda Revolucionaria has uniquely influenced PCV behavior. From its inception in 1960, it pictured itself "to the Left" of the PCV. This competition for spokesmanship of the extreme Left in national politics was fundamental in forcing the PCV into the decision for violence which they took early in 1962. Similarly, PCV abandonment of violence in 1966-67 encountered strong resistance from the MIR elements who wanted to continue the guerrilla war, and who did do so even after the PCV withdrew.

PRESSURES WITHIN COMMUNIST RANKS

Pressures from within Communist ranks exerted major forces on the Venezuelan Communist movement in the early 1940's and in the early 1960's.

During the former period, factionalism was rife within Communist ranks. One group wanted to collaborate closely with the government of General Isaías Medina Angarita, the other advocated a less compromising relationship with that regime. These differences split the party ranks and led to formation of the Partido Comunista de Venezuela and the Partido Comunista Unitario, which later became the Partido Revolucionario Proletario (Comunista).

The second period in which internal pressures were a determining factor in the behavior of the Venezuelan Communists was during the Betancourt regime in the early 1960's. It seems clear that most of the older leaders were against abandoning the policy of strong but non-violent opposition to the Betancourt government and the objective of winning support in labor, peasant, and professional organizations from those who would become disillusioned with the Acción Democrática-Copei regime. However, they were confronted by a younger leadership that drew support from recruits brought into the party after the fall of Pérez Jiménez and was especially strong among university and high school members and followers of the party. This faction advocated force as the means

217

to overthrow the Betancourt government, and the older leaders acceded to that policy.

There is some evidence that after the successful election in December 1963 signalled the failure of the urban terrorismcampaign, the older leadership urged a more peaceful policy. However, subjected to open threats of personal violence if they insisted on this revision of the party's strategy, they demurred at that time. Only when the guerrilla warfare undertaken early in 1964 also failed were the older leaders able to win over enough of the younger element to force abandonment of the guerrilla campaign.

NON-NATIONAL DETERMINANTS OF PCV BEHAVIOR

The only non-Venezuelan factor to influence appreciably the behavior of the Venezuelan party has been that of other Communist parties. The Communist Party of the Soviet Union, and since 1961 the Communist Party of Cuba, have been the most significant influences.

For many years the Communist Party of Venezuela was principally influenced by the CPSU. It was a member of the CPSU-dominated Communist International. In the late 1940's and early 1950's it was associated with the Cominform, which was also dominated by the Communist Party of the USSR.

Two examples of the influence of the CPSU on the Venezuelan party are its behavior during World War II and its withdrawal from guerrilla war in 1966-67.

The PCV followed the line of the world Communist movement, determined by the CPSU, during World War II. Between the outbreak of the conflict and the German attack on the Soviet Union, the Venezuelan Communists were "neutralists," arguing that the workers of Venezuela had no interest in who won the war. After the Nazi invasion of the USSR, the Allied cause became almost a crusade for the Venezuelan Communists. This change in attitude toward the war was undoubtedly of key importance in determining the PCV position on internal affairs in Venezuela. Communist parties throughout Latin America threw their support to any government which proclaimed itself on the Allied side, regardless of the nature of that government or its domestic affairs policies. The PCV was no exception: it was principally for this reason that the Communists supported the Medina Angarita government after 1941.

The CPSU continued to influence the PCV even into the 1960's, although we cannot be sure whether it actively tried to dissuade the PCV from taking the road to violence in 1962. However, it is clear that Soviet influence was brought to bear when a vigorous controversy started in 1965 over withdrawal from the guerrilla effort. (We have noted Jesús Faria's visit to Moscow immediately upon his release from prison by the Leoni government.) Moreover, the PCV took pains to maintain friendly relations with the Soviet-influenced Communist parties throughout the period of its experiment with violence.

The influence of the Cuban Communist Party certainly conflicted with the CPSU in this controversy. Castro's influence had loomed large even before he had declared Cuba part of the world Communist camp. The Cuban Revolution had aroused the imagination especially of younger members and leaders of the PCV. An undetermined number of young Venezuelan Communists were sent to Cuba for various kinds of training, and the Castro regime early brought its influence to bear upon them and other leftists (from MIR and the left-wing of URD) to overthrow the Betancourt government by force.

When the PCV reconsidered its policy of violence after 1965, the Cuban party undoubtedly wielded its influence toward continuing the guerrilla war. When the Venezuelans finally took the decision to end their guerrilla activities, the Cuban party leadership vehemently attacked the PCV leaders, and announced that it would continue to support the guerrilla leader Douglas Bravo, who had been expelled from the PCV for his insistence on continuing the policy of violence.

In this controversy over PCV strategy, with the Cuban and Soviet parties in direct conflict, the loyalty of the older PCV leaders to the CPSU must have carried greater weight in determining the ultimate decision.

The Partido Comunista de Venezuela was founded by a group of rebellious students in the midst of the struggle against the tyranny of Juan Vicente Gómez. Its first opportunity to operate more or less legally came with the death of Gómez in December 1935. From then until the middle of 1937 it was free to organize, and in that period the PCV first developed its roots among the members of the newly established labor movement, which it was to control for somewhat less than a decade.

During most of its history the PCV has had little to distinguish it from similar parties in other Latin American countries. So long as the Communist International existed, the PCV followed its line loyally and without question. A bit later, it followed the directives of the Cominform as it had those of the Comintern.

The PCV has remained a minority group in national politics, and until the early 1960's it evinced little influence or importance in the Communist movement in Latin America as a whole. Its domestic strength was insufficient to give it much prestige outside Venezuela, and its leaders were not particularly renowned among their foreign confreres for their intellectual brilliance or oratorical prowess.

However, the resort to violence by the Partido Comunista de Venezuela in 1962 gave it a unique role among the Communist parties of the hemisphere. During 1962 and 1963 it joined with the Movimiento de Izquierda Revolucionaria in launching a campaign of urban terrorism in Caracas and other major cities, and scattered guerrilla activity in rural areas. When this failed in its apparent aim of forcing a military coup against the Betancourt government and when it did not prevent the election of December 1963, the Communists and their allies regrouped their forces and launched what was projected to be a long-term guerrilla war.

The Communist Party, the Movimiento de Izquierda Revolucionaria, and a dissident group from the Unión Republicana Democrática had formed the Frente de Liberación Nacional (FLN) as the political united front to lead the terrorist and guerrilla campaigns, and had given the label of Fuerzas Armadas de Liberación Nacional (FALN) to the groups actually carrying out these campaigns. However, by 1965 the leaders of the FLN and the FALN, including Douglas Bravo, a member of the Political Bureau of the PCV, were manifesting an independence of the parties which had sponsored them—particularly of the PCV.

This independent attitude, expressed in a reorganization of the FLN and FALN leadership by the guerrilla leaders without consultation with the Political Bureau of the PCV, served as an excuse for the first open break between the Communists and what had been their guerrilla arm. At the same time, a controversy was brewing within the party between those who urged continuing the struggle in the mountains and those who stood for a return to peaceful and constitutional procedures. The upshot of this dispute was the decision to stop guerrilla activities. Douglas Bravo and other guerrilla leaders were expelled from the Partido Comunista de Venezuela, and the Central Committee resolved to return to electoral activities, and to participate, if possible, in the presidential and legislative election of 1968.

This decision precipitated a polemic between the leaders of the PCV and Fidel Castro and the Communist Party of Cuba. It underscored a growing split between Castro and groups like the MIR, the FLN and the FALN on the one hand, and the orthodox Communist parties of Latin America on the other.

The experience of the Partido Comunista de Venezuela, particularly during the last half dozen years, provides valuable object lessons to the other Communist parties of the hemisphere and to their opponents.

On the one hand, at least a tentative conclusion can be drawn that the kind of urban and rural violence which the Venezuelan Communists used is not apt to succeed against a well-entrenched, popularly elected, reformist regime. A principal source of strength for the Bentacourt-Leoni regime has been the loyalty it inspires from most of the urban population and from the overwhelming majority of the peasants. The violence in the cities tended to turn the organized labor movement against the Communists until their influence was nearly destroyed in a sector which they had penetrated with some success during the immediately preceding years. In the rural areas, the peasantry proved much more likely to inform on the Communist guerrillas, or even round them up themselves, than to join them.

The reasons for these responses are not hard to find.

The Acción Democrática regime has been carrying on
since 1959 a democratic revolution that is transforming
the society, the economy, and the politics of Venezuela.
It has provided 140,000 farm families with land of their
own; it has brought running water, electricity, schools,
medical dispensaries to small towns and hamlets throughout the interior. It has increased agricultural production
and developed manufacturing. It has established as a rule
the settlement of labor-management difficulties through
collective bargaining.

All of these measures, carried out under a system of
constitutional democracy, have done much to strengthen
that system. To the extent that they have kept the regime
relatively popular, they have also reenforced Acción Democrática. But more important, those citizens who have
become disillusioned with AD have turned to democratic
opposition parties—Copei, Unión Republicana Democrática,
and even smaller groups like Admiral Larrazábal's Frente
Democrático Popular and the extremist but democratic
Partido Revolucionario de la Izquierda Nacionalista—rather
than to the PCV, which has been seeking to overthrow not
only Acción Democratica but the whole system of democratic constitutional government.

A second lesson to be learned from PCV history is
that its resort to violence strengthened the support of the
democratic regime by the country's armed forces. The
military leaders realized the danger to the armed forces
as an institution from the guerrilla and terrorist activities
of the Communists and their allies. Their nationalistic
sentiments were also outraged by the evident help the Cuban
regime gave to the terrorists and guerrillas.

Venezuelan military leaders in general have felt that
their own best interests and those of the nation lie in defending the reformist democratic regime. They refused

to do what the terrorists apparently wanted them to do in 1962 and 1963—overthrow the Betancourt government—because they realized that a military dictatorship would be very unpopular, giving the Communists and MIR a chance to rally the people against it, and guerrilla war under such circumstances would be a disaster. The best insurance against this was for the military to give full backing to the civilian government, which enjoyed popular support.

A third moral to be drawn from PCV experience with violence is that failure exacts a very high cost. The Communist failure to induce the military to oust the Betancourt government, and the failure of the guerrilla warfare to develop the proportions of a real civil war, had brought the PCV in four years to a worse situation than it had endured since the days of the López Contreras regime (1935-41). It had lost almost every labor union formerly under its control, most of its following in the professional organizations, and many of what peasant adherents it had had before 1962. Its members had been more thoroughly purged from public employment than perhaps ever before. Even its influence in the student movement had been reduced. In the general political picture, the PCV had become a pariah to be shunned by other political groups.

In addition to this decimation of PCV influence, the party leaders found their own organization in a shambles. They complained of lethargy among members and of their failure even to pay party dues regularly, of various organizational failures in subsidiary groups of the party hierarchy.

Other Communist parties in Latin America are well aware of the catastrophe the Partido Comunista de Venesuela has suffered from the failure of its appeal to force.

This knowledge undoubtedly has strengthened the resistance of Communist parties throughout the hemisphere to the insistence of Fidel Castro that the only acceptable road to power for Communists in Latin America is through terrorism and guerrilla warfare. This resistance was demostrated in July 1967, when only a handful of orthodox Communist parties sent delegates to the founding Congress of the Latin American Solidarity Organization(OLAS), held in Havana and called by Castro to stimulate and direct insurrections throughout Latin America. The few who did attend took a position against Castro's dogma that prosecution of civil war was mandatory for anyone who claimed to be a Communist. The PCV quite pointedly was not invited to the Havana Congress.

By early 1967 the Partido Comunista de Venezuela had definitely decided to return to operating within the country's democratic constitutional framework. It is still too early to predict what success the PCV will have in forming alliances with other extreme leftist groups which are also using constitutional procedures. Nor can one make any valid assessment of the Communists' ability to recoup some of their lost influence in the labor movement, in peasant organizations, and in other occupational groups.

The future of the PCV depends in large measure on what happens in the general political situation. If progress continues in the years immediately ahead toward establishment of a strong economic and social basis for political democracy, it seems unlikely that the Communists will become a major factor in Venezuelan political life. Under these circumstances, the organized labor movement, the peasant leadership, and the professional organizations will probably remain largely in the hands of Acción Democrática and Copei, the parties which are the

principal agents in a program of social reform, nationalism, and rapid economic development within the framework of political democracy.

The Communists are even likely to encounter trouble
with the one group in which they managed to maintain their
influence throughout the guerrilla period—the students.
The alliance they have had since 1959-60 with Movimiento
de Izquierda Revolucionaria will probably not survive the
cleavage of opinion between the two parties over the issue
of continued violence. Since the alliance with the MIR is
unlikely to be soon succeeded by an agreement with any
other major element in the student field, the PCV can ex-
pect their representation in leading bodies of the student
movement to decline, at least temporarily.

Only if the military indulge once again in their old
habit of overthrowing constituted governments does it
seem that the Communists could become a significant
factor in national politics. Such an eventuality would undoubtedly demoralize the democratic parties, particularly
Acción Democrática, and would give the Communists a
chance to assume leadership in a widely backed effort to
overthrow an unpopular regime. However, with each
passing month the likelihood of such a development tends
to decline. If President Raúl Leoni is able to hand over
his presidential sash to a democratically elected successor,
Venezuela will be well on the way to establishing a tradition of democratic government. Each president who com-
pletes his term makes it that much more difficult from a
psychological point of view for the military to oust his
successor.

Ironically, the continuance of the Castro government
in Cuba tends to strengthen the democratic regime in Venezuela, and hence reduce the possibility of the Communists'
gaining widespread support: the spectre of the Castro

government only two hundred miles away should constrain the military in Venezuela from plotting against the regime in power. On the other hand, Castro's overthrow might well remove a major impediment to barracks conspiracy.

The Partido Comunista de Venezuela seems to be effectively prevented from making any dramatic headway in the foreseeable future. It will spend a long time paying for its recklessness in advocating force as the road to power—and for its even more devastating failure to make this appeal to force successful.

NOTES

I HISTORY OF VENEZUELAN COMMUNIST PARTY

1 Robert J. Alexander, Communism in Latin America (New Brunswick, New Jersey: Rutgers University Press, 1957), p. 254.

2 Damaso Rojas, "Las 'Memorias' de Gustavo Machado," Elite (Caracas), May 16, 1964.

3 Alexander, p. 254

4 Robert J. Alexander, Prophets of the Revolution, (New York: Macmillan, 1962), chapter on Rómulo Betancourt entitled, "Rómulo Betancourt: Statesman of the Andes."

5 Interview with Juan Bautista Fuenmayor, Secretary General of Partido Comunista de Venezuela, in Caracas, July 29, 1947.

6 Alexander, Communism in Latin America, p. 255.

7 John D. Martz, Acción Democrática, Evolution of a Modern Political Party in Venezuela, (Princeton: Princeton University Press, 1966), pp. 27-37.

8 Ibid., pp. 44-45.

9 Alexander, Prophets of the Revolution, chapter on Rómulo Betancourt.

10   Martz, pp. 40-41.

11   Alexander, Communism in Latin America, p. 256.

12   Ibid., p. 258.

13   Ibid., p. 257.

14   Ibid., p. 259.

15   Ibid., p. 264.

16   Fundamentos, ("theoretical" journal of Partido Socialista Popular [Communist Party] of Cuba), Havana, August 1947.

17   Rómulo Betancourt, Venezuela, Politica y Petroleo (Mexico, D. F.: Fundo de Cultura Economica, 1955), p. 286.

18   Ibid., pp. 303-309.

19   Ibid., p. 412.

20   Ibid., p. 413.

21   Ibid., p. 419.

22   Ibid., p. 418.

23   Ibid., pp. 431-432.

24   Ibid., p. 439.

25   Ibid., p. 300.

26   Ibid.

27 Alexander, Communism in Latin America, p. 263.

28 Ibid.

29 Betancourt, p. 338.

30 Ibid., pp. 386-389.

31 Ibid., p. 397.

32 Martz, p. 75.

33 Alexander, Communism in Latin America, p. 264.

34 Ibid.

35 Venezuela Democrática, (exile publication of Acción
    Democrática), Mexico, D. F., January-February 1956.

36 Fuenmayor interview.

37 Alexander, Communism in Latin America, p. 260.

38 Ibid., p. 263.

39 Ibid.

40 Jesús Faria, Informe del Comité Central al Tercer
    Congreso del Partido Comunista de Venezuela, a
    Cargo de Jesús Faria, Secretario General del PCV,
    May 1961, p. 4.

41 Alexander, Communism in Latin America, p. 267.

42 Ibid., p. 268.

43 Ibid., p. 269.

44 Faria, p. 4.

45 Diario de la Marina, daily newspaper, Havana, May 14, 1950.

46 Faria, loc. cit.

47 Ibid.

48 Ibid.

49 Ibid., p. 5.

50 Ibid.

51 Ibid.

52 Alexander, loc. cit., p. 266.

53 Faria, p. 7.

54 Ibid., p. 8.

55 Interview with Cruz Villegas, trade union leader of Communist Party, in Caracas, August 18, 1959.

56 Interview with Rómulo Betancourt, leader of Acción Democrática, in Piscataway, N.J., August 11, 1957.

57 Faria, p. 9.

58 Ibid.

59 Ministerio de Agricultura y Cría, Comisión de Reforma Agraria, Reforma Agraria, (Caracas, 1959).

60 Martz, pp. 105-6.

II THE PCV'S EXPERIMENT WITH VIOLENCE

1 Faria, p. 11.

2 Ibid.

3 Ibid. , p. 12.

4 Ibid.

5 Carlos Andrés Pérez, "Exposición Al Pais del Minis-
tro de Relaciones Interiores, Doctor Carlos Andrés
Pérez, Con Motivo del Decreto de Suspensión de Ac-
tividades de los Partidos Comunista y Movimiento de
Izquierda Revolucionaria, " press release, Oficina
de Prensa y Relaciones de la Presidencia de la Republica, (Caracas, May 10, 1962).

6 Faria, pp. 12-13.

7 Ibid. , p. 26.

8 Ibid. , p. 27.

9 Ibid.

10 La Republica (Acción Democrática-oriented daily),
Caracas, July 20, 1961.

11 Robert J. Alexander, The Venezuelan Democratic
Revolution, A Profile of the Regime of Rómulo Betancourt, (New Brunswick: Rutgers University Press,
1964), p. 169.

12 Rómulo Betancourt, VI Mensaje Presidencial, 7 de
Marzo de 1964, (Caracas, 1964), p. 32.

13 Ibid. , p. 35.

14 Ibid. , p. 36.

15 Ibid. , pp. 39-40.

16 Faria, p. 26.

17 Pérez speech.

18 A full account of the extremists' terrorist campaign can be found in Seis Años de Agresión, a booklet issued by the Oficina Central de Informacion, Caracas, 1967.

19 See speech by Carlos Andrés Pérez in La Subversión Extremista en Venezuela, Publicacione de la Francción Parlamentaria de Acción Democrática, (Caracas, 1964).

20 Interview with Valmore Acevedo, leader of Copei, in Princeton, N. J. , April 24, 1965.

21 Norman Gall, "The Continental Revolution, " New Leader, April 12, 1965, p. 3.

22 See speech by Salom Meza in La Subversión Extremista p. 84.

23 See Confidencial, Caracas, no. 18, April 29, 1965.

24 Anchova interview, and interview with Dr. Rafael Caldera, head of Copei, in Caracas, July 28, 1965.

25 Pérez speech (1964), p. 43.

26 See Confidencial, Caracas, no. 1, May 25, 1964.

27 See Confidencial, Caracas, no. 32, August 1966.

28 Ibid.

29 See Confidencial, Caracas, no. 35, October 1966.

30 See speech by Fidel Castro, March 13, 1967, reported in Gramma, Havana, March 19, 1967.

31 See Confidencial, Caracas, no. 34, September 1966.

32 See speech by Fidel Castro, op. cit.

33 Ibid.

34 Ibid.

35 Ibid.

36 Talton Ray, ''The Political Life of the Venezuelan Barrios,'' [unpublished], p. 192.

37 Ibid. , p. 196.

III THE STRUCTURE, ROLE, AND ORGANIZATION OF THE VENEZUELAN COMMUNIST PARTY

1 ''Estudio Sobre el Partido Comunista de Venezuela Basado en Documentos del Partido'' (unpublished study, Dirección General de Policía, Caracas, 1963, hereafter referred to as Digepol Study), p. 14.

2 Ibid. , p. 4.

3 Ibid.

4   Ibid., p. 6.

5   Ibid., p. 7.

6   Ibid., pp. 7-10.

7   Ibid., p. 22.

8   Ibid., pp. 24-26.

9   Ibid., p. 32.

10 Ibid.

11 Ibid., p. 34.

12 Ibid., p. 27.

13 Ibid., pp. 29-30.

14 Confidencial, Caracas, no. 2, May 31, 1964.

15 Ibid., no. 14, January 21, 1965.

16 Ibid., no. 12, November 10, 1964.

IV THE VENEZUELAN ENVIRONMENT

1   Salvador de Madariaga, Bolivar, Pellegrini and
    Cudahy, New York, 1952.

2   United Nations, Economic Commission for Latin
    America, Economic Survey Latin America 1963,
    (New York, 1965), pp. 106 and 178.

3 Guillermo García Ponce, Introducción a la Politica Venezolana, (Caracas, January 1961).

4 Banco Central de Venezuela, Informe Economico, Banco Central, 1965, Caracas, 1966, p. 475.

5 Raúl Leoni, II Mensaje Presidencial, (Caracas, 1965), Table 4, p. 8.

V PCV'S CONFLICT AND INTEGRATION WITH THE VENEZUELAN ENVIRONMENT

1 Alexander, Communism in Latin America, p. 266.

2 García Ponce, p. 26.

3 Ibid., p. 27.

4 Eduardo Machado, Petroleo en Venezuela, (Caracas, n. d.), Distribuidora Magrija, C.A., p. 26. This pamphlet reprints part of the speech by Machado in 1947.

5 Ibid., pp. 21-22.

6 García Ponce, p. 53.

7 Digepol Study, p. 40.

8 Martz, p. 270.

9 Digepol Study, p. 39.

10 Ibid.

11 Ibid., pp. 40-41.

12 General José R. Gabaldón, Documento de Paz y Libertad, (Caracas, 1965).

13 El Nacional, Caracas, May 19, 1968.

14 Cited in La Republica, August 19, 1968.

VI THE PCV'S RELATIONS WITH
OTHER COMMUNIST PARTIES

1 García Ponce, p. 23.

2 Faria, p. 21.

3 Castro speech, March 13, 1967.

4 El Amigo del Pueblo, (Cuban exile periodical), NYC, March 1967.

5 Marcha, (Leftist Weekly), Montevideo, August 11, 1967.

6 International Socialist Review, (U. S. Trotskyite periodical), New York, November-December 1967, p. 29.

7 Fuenmayor interview.

8 Interview with Earl Browder, ex-Secretary-General of Communist Party of the United States, in Yonkers, New York, March 23, 1953.

9 Fundamentos, August 1947.

10 Alexander, Communism in Latin America, p. 260.

11 Escuela Sindical Ezequiel Zamora, (Caracas, n. d.).

12 El Amigo del Pueblo, March 1967.

13 New York Times, April 11, 1965.

BIBLIOGRAPHICAL NOTE

The reader will find listed below all the sources of material cited in these pages. For background material and for drawing judgments about the Partido Comunista de Venezuela and its history, the author has also relied on interviews with Communists and others which are not mentioned here, on observations at meetings, at Communist headquarters, and the like; such sources are sometimes difficult to cite. In this Bibliographical Note, we have therefore limited ourselves to listing those sources to which we make attribution in the monograph itself.

The reader will note that for some of the historical material, the author has relied on other books he has previously written. This apparent egotism will, we hope, be pardoned. The reader is invited to look at those books if he is interested in finding the sources from which the statements concerned are drawn. It seemed more logical to list the published books, which are in English, than to go back and list the original sources from which statements or judgments had been drawn for an earlier work.

BOOKS AND PAMPHLETS

Robert J. Alexander, Communism in Latin America, Rutgers University Press, New Brunswick, New Jersey, 1957--A general survey, now somewhat dated, of the Communist parties of Latin America. It analyzes them in general terms of leadership, influence in organized labor, etc., and on a country-by-country basis.

Robert J. Alexander, Prophets of the Revolution, Macmillan, New York, 1962--This book contains profiles of a dozen important Latin American political leaders of the last generation, including a chapter on Rómulo Betancourt.

Robert J. Alexander, The Venezuelan Democratic Revolution, A Profile of the Regime of Rómulo Betancourt, Rutgers University Press, New Brunswick, N.J. 1964-- A general and fairly thorough study of the Betancourt administration of 1959.

Rómulo Betancourt, Venezuela, Politica y Petroleo, Fundo de Cultura Economica, Mexico, DF, 1955--A study of Venezuelan affairs from the end of the Gomez regime to virtually the date of publication, with particular attention to the first Acción Democrática administration of 1945-48. It has valuable statistical material on that period, and judgments by Betancourt on what was accomplished.

Escuela Sindical Ezequiel Zamora, Caracas, n. d. --A pamphlet put out in the name of one of the Communist training schools in Caracas in the early 1950's. It consists of articles from various international Communist publications.

Fracción Parlamentaria de Acción Democrática, La Subversión Extremista en Venezuela, Caracas, 1964-- This pamphlet contains speeches by three AD deputies, Carlos Andres Pérez, Luis Piñerua Ordáz, and Salom Meza, on the terrorist and guerrilla activities of the PCV and MIR.

General José R. Gabaldón, Documento de Paz y Libertad, Caracas, 1965--This pamphlet, published by one of the Communist front organizations of Venezuela, is a statement to the Inter-American Conference in Rio de Janeiro in 1965.

Guillermo García Ponce, Introducción a la Politica Venezolana, Caracas, January 1961--A fascinating pamphlet written by a member of the PCV Political Bureau and presenting the Party's view of the Venezuelan situation, and the objectives of the PCV, about a year before the resort to violence.

Oficina Central de Información, Seis Años de Agresión, Caracas, n.d. (1967)--A documented study of the whole campaign of terror and guerrilla war from 1962 on, with names, dates, and other relevant information. Published in both Spanish and English.

Eduardo Machado, Petroleo en Venezuela, Distribuidora Magrija, C.A., Caracas, n.d. --This is a statement in pamphlet form of the party's position on the petroleum question by a member of the PCV's Politburo.

Salvador de Madariaga, Bolivar, Pellegrini and Cudahy, New York, 1952 --A distinguished biography of the father of Venezuelan independence, written largely to deflate the so-called "Black Legend" about the Spaniards in Spanish America.

John D. Martz, Acción Democrática, Evolution of a Modern Political Party in Venezuela, Princeton University Press, Princeton, N.J., 1966--An expert study of the history, organization, and activity of the major party of Venezuela.

REPORTS, YEARBOOKS, ETC.

Banco Central de Venezuela, Informe Economico, Banco

Central 1965, Caracas--An annual survey not only of Central Bank operations, but of many other aspects of the national economy.

Rómulo Betancourt, VI Mensaje Presidencial, 7 de Marzo de 1964, Caracas, 1964--The last annual report to Congress by President Betancourt, containing much summary data on the accomplishments of his administration.

Economic Commission for Latin America, Economic Survey of Latin America 1964, United Nations, 1966--One of the periodic studies by the ECLA of various Latin American national economies.

Jesús Faria, Informe del Comité Central al Tercer Congreso del Partido Comunista de Venezuela, a Cargo de Jesús Faria, Secretario General del PCV, May 1961--Invaluable report on the Communist Party's activities between 1948 and 1961.

Rául Leoni, II Mensaje Presidencial, 11 de Marzo de 1965, Caracas, 1965--President Leoni's second annual report to Congress; contains much information on events and government policies during this period.

Ministerio de Agricultura y Cría, Comisión de Reforma Agraria, Reforma Agraria--The multi-volumed report of the Agrarian Reform Commission established during the Larrazábal administration. It was submitted in 1959 to the Betancourt administration, and contains detailed studies of the state of agriculture and landholding in Venezuela at that time.

United Nations, Demographic Yearbook--Annual publication of UN, giving extensive details on population and population trends throughout the world.

U. S. Department of State, Bureau of Intelligence Reports, World Strength of Communist Organizations, --An annual survey of the Communist movement.

PERIODICALS

Communist International--A monthly periodical of the Comintern; contained interesting and valuable articles on the Communist movement in various parts of the world.

Confidencial, Caracas--A publication of the Ministry of Internal Affairs during 1964-66, comprising captured documents of the Communist and MIR parties and of their guerrilla and terrorist groups.

Elite--Weekly magazine of Caracas, for popular distribution; contains some political articles.

El Nacional--Independent daily of Caracas, whose columns are open to people of virtually all political tendencies, including the Communists.

El Amigo del Pueblo--Small periodical issued by a Cuban exile group in New York. Keeps track of relations of Castro regime with other Communist parties.

Fundamentos--Organ of the Partido Socialista Popular, the old Communist Party of Cuba; contained interesting articles on other Latin American Communist parties.

International Socialist Review, New York--Organ of the official Trotskyite Socialist Workers Party, pro-Castro. Contains material on Leftist groups in Latin America from time to time.

La Republica--Pro-Acción Democrática daily paper in Caracas.

Marcha--Leftist weekly in Montevideo. Recent issues have had considerable material on the Organización Latino Americana de Solidaridad founding Congress in Havana.

New Leader--Political weekly of New York City; sometimes contains interesting articles on Latin America.

New York Times--Still the best general source on Latin American affairs in the United States.

Noticias de Venezuela--Exile organ of Partido Comunista de Venezuela in 1950's, published in Mexico.

Patria Nueva--Organ of the National Executive Commission of Juventud Comunista of Venezuela in 1950's.

Peking Review--Chinese periodical which keeps close track of world-wide pro-Chinese Communist groups.

P. R. P. Comunista--Publication of "Black" Communists in 1947-48.

Tribuna Popular--Daily newspaper of Partido Comunista de Venezuela, in 1948 and again in 1959-62.

Venezuela Democrática--Exile periodical of Acción Democrática in 1950's, published in Mexico.

World Marxist Review--More or less official organ of pro-Soviet Communist Parties; contains interesting and valuable information on these parties.

UNPUBLISHED MATERIAL

Dirección General de Policía, "Estudio Sobre el Partido
    Comunista de Venezuela Basado en Documentos del
    Partido"--Valuable study of various documents--many
    quoted in extenso--captured by police from Communist
    Party of Venezuela.

Press Release, President's Office, "Exposición Al Pais
    del Ministro de Relaciones Interiores Doctor Carlos
    Andrés Pérez, Con Motivo del Decreto de Suspensión
    de Actividades de los Partidos Communista y Movimiento
    de Izquierda Revolucionaria"--Contains interesting
    information on beginnings of terrorist campaign, dated
    May 10, 1962.

Press Release, President's Office, "Exposición del Presi-
    dente de la Republica, Señor Rómulo Betancourt, Con
    Motivo de la Acción Insurreccional de Carúpano, "
    May 9, 1962--Information on origins and nature of
    leftist revolt at Carúpano, May 1962.

Talton Ray, "The Political Life of the Venezuelan Bar-
    rios"--As yet unpublished study, with exceedingly
    useful information on the political trends and develop-
    ments in the shanty-town areas of Caracas and other
    major cities.

INTERVIEWS

Valmore Acevedo, former deputy of Copei, former Gover-
    nor of State of Táchira under Betancourt, in Princeton,
    New Jersey, April 24, 1965.

Rómulo Betancourt, in Piscataway, New Jersey, August 11,
    1957.

Earl Browder, former Secretary General of Communist
Party of the United States, in Yonkers, N.Y., March
23, 1953.

Rafael Caldera, Secretary General and principal leader
of Copei Party, in Caracas, July 28, 1965.

Juan Bautista Fuenmayor, then Secretary General and
deputy of Partido Comunista de Venezuela, in Caracas,
July 29, 1947.

Cruz Villegas, one of major trade union leaders of Partido
Comunista de Venezuela, and later member of Central
Committee of Party, in Caracas, August 18, 1959.